Eat! Enjoy!

Eat! Enjoy!

The 101 Best Jewish Recipes in America

HONEY AND LARRY ZISMAN

ST. MARTIN'S GRIFFIN NEW YORK

For Jordana, Jackie, Craig,
Samantha, Sean, Emily, and Corina.
May you always Enjoy! Enjoy! your heritage.

Book design by Richard Oriolo
Illustrations by Michael Storrings

Library of Congress Cataloging-in-Publication Data

Zisman, Honey.
Eat! enjoy!: the 101 best Jewish recipes in America / Honey and Larry Zisman.
p. cm.
ISBN 0-312-25381-8
1. Cookery, Jewish. I. Zisman, Larry. II. Title.

TX724 .Z57 2000
641.5'676—dc21   99-089299

First Edition: March 2000

10   9   8   7   6   5   4   3   2   1

Contents

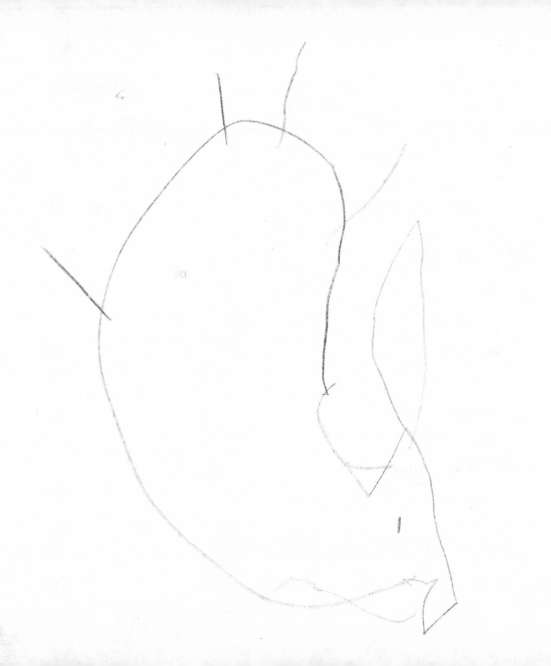

Eat! Enjoy!
An Introduction

For nearly six thousand years, through good times and bad—whether gathered in the Land of Israel or scattered throughout the world in the Diaspora—the Jewish people have remained united and connected to one another with deeply held religious beliefs, a strong ethical and moral code, shared historical experiences, and enduring feelings of cultural identity.

But there is even something more that binds the Jewish people together.

That one additional cohesive bond among the Jews is food—good food, great food, and lots and lots of it. And even more food, if you please.

Food may be nutrition, food may be life, but to Jewish people food is also a gift; food is a celebration; and food is, almost, who we are.

To satisfy this interest—no, this obsession—with food, Jewish people have enthusiastically developed a wide range of dishes to be lovingly prepared, heartily eaten, thoroughly enjoyed, and greatly praised . . . and woe to whoever fails to join in.

The Jewish interest in food can be seen in a multitude of restaurants, delis, hotels, and resorts; in food stores, large and small, offering kosher, kosher-style, and traditional foods; and in millions of homes throughout the world—regardless of whatever national culture—where preparing and eating food is akin to a religious experience.

We ourselves are enthusiastic participants in this enduring ardor for eating. Larry's grandmother continued to make knishes well into her 90s, still rolling out the dough by hand so uniformly thin that you could easily read the *Forward* (the Yiddish language newspaper that educated and informed a whole generation of immigrants) through the dough.

Golda Meir was entertained in Honey's grandmother's home right here in New Jersey and enjoyed the chicken matzoh ball soup that was a Kligerman family legend, along with the rich and joyful foods from the Kligerman family dairy that was founded by Honey's grandparents.

And Honey herself makes challah, potato latkes, noodle kugel, tzimmes (different medleys of meats, potatoes, and fruits), and wine cake that never fail to delight our guests. She also makes hamantashen for Purim—poppy seed, lekvar (prune), and jelly—as delicious as any.

But enough about us and what we eat . . . and eat . . . and eat. It is time to turn to what Jewish people throughout the United States make, eat, and enjoy. From traditional recipes handed down from generation to generation, brought from country to country, to new creations prepared just for the holidays, there is a vast cornucopia of Jewish dishes out there just waiting to be collected and disseminated for everyone—not just immediate family members and close friends—to enjoy.

And that is what we have done. The "Jewish Dishes, So Delicious" recipe contest attracted a variety and a multitude of recipes from throughout the country and made judging this contest one of life's great joys—a true simcha that we wish we could have shared with everyone.

You should know it was not easy, it was not quick, and it was not without many hard choices to be able to pick just 101 of the best from all those delicious, interesting, and desirable Jewish dishes from throughout the United States. But a sense of mission prevailed and we did choose the 101 best and want to share them with everyone who wants to enjoy the best of Jewish cooking.

It was truly a mitzvah.

There was one dilemma, however. Since our friends and relatives were prohibited from participating in the contest, we could not include them as contest winners. But what about all their great dishes we've enjoyed over the years?

The solution, worthy of King Solomon, is a separate section in our book with the best recipes from some of our relatives and friends.

So it is, the best of the best and then some more.

As our mothers and grandmothers—and generations of mothers and grand-mothers before them—kept telling us:

Enjoy! Enjoy!

Authors' note: Since there are no inherently unkosher ingredients in any of the recipes in this book, all the recipes can be prepared kosher using strictly kosher ingredients. When necessary, nondairy ingredients can be used in place of any dairy items.

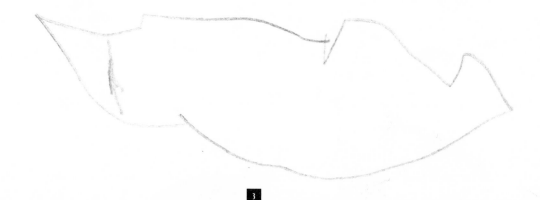

The Winning Recipes

Challah French Toast Herman Ivanson * Tempe, Arizona

4 eggs	*8 1- to 1½-inch slices of challah*
¾ to 1 cup milk	*Cinnamon Sugar (recipe follows)*
dash of salt	*maple syrup, heated*
1 teaspoon vanilla	*cherry pie filling, heated, optional*

- Beat eggs. Add milk, salt, and vanilla.
- Thoroughly soak slices of challah in egg and milk mixture, first on one side and turning over to soak the other side.
- Fry challah slices in a greased electric frying pan, set on French Toast setting, for about 4 minutes on each side, to desired doneness.
- Sprinkle with cinnamon sugar and serve with heated maple syrup.
- For a special treat, top with heated cherry pie filling.

Yield: 8 slices

Cinnamon Sugar

1 tablespoon cinnamon
½ cup sugar

- Thoroughly mix together cinnamon and sugar.

Almond Blintz Pancakes Gail Jablonski * Ogden, Utah

2 cups flour

3 tablespoons sugar

¾ teaspoon salt

2 cups fat-free sour cream

2 cups fat-free cottage cheese

8 eggs, beaten

1½ teaspoons almond flavoring

heated syrup

confectioners' sugar, optional

- In a large bowl, mix together flour, sugar, and salt. Add in sour cream, cottage cheese, and eggs, one at a time. Stir in almond flavoring.
- Pour enough batter for a 3½-inch circle onto a greased hot griddle.
- Cook until bubbles form. Flip over for a few minutes, until both sides are cooked to desired doneness.
- Remove from griddle and serve with heated syrup.
- Dust with confectioners' sugar, if desired.

Yield: approximately 30 pancakes

The first kosher cookbook published in the United States was called *Jewish Cookery* and was written by Esther Levy, née Jacobs. It was printed in Philadelphia in 1871.

Lox and Asparagus
Strata Cindy L. Bures, Harvey Luber ✳ Josolyn House Bed & Breakfast, Little Rock, Arkansas

¾ pound thin asparagus stalks, cut into
   3-inch pieces

6 large pieces of sourdough bread

butter or margarine

½ cup sharp Cheddar cheese, crumbled
   (can use low fat)

6 slices lox

4 eggs or 1 cup Egg Beaters

1½ cups milk (can use skim)

1 scallion, finely chopped

garlic salt, to taste

pepper, to taste

cinnamon

- Preheat oven to 325° F. Butter a 7 x 11-inch glass dish.
- Cook asparagus until just tender but still firm. Drain and set aside.
- Cut ends off sourdough bread and cut in two, resulting in 12 serving-size squares. Lightly brush with butter.
- Place 6 bread pieces, buttered side up, in the buttered glass dish. Sprinkle with half the Cheddar cheese. Layer each piece of bread with lox and asparagus. Cover with remaining 6 pieces of bread. Set aside.
- In a bowl, lightly beat eggs. Add milk, scallion, garlic salt, and pepper. Pour over bread in dish. Sprinkle cinnamon over top.
- Bake uncovered for 50 minutes.
- Remove from oven and sprinkle with remaining cheese.
- Return to oven and bake for 10 minutes more.
- Remove from oven and let cool for 10 minutes.

- Recipe can be doubled and made the night before, covered, and refrigerated.
- If desired, serve with blackberry muffins and fresh fruit.

Yield: 6 servings

When is lox not lox?

According to purists, lox is not lox when it is Nova Scotia smoked salmon.

People who are eating Nova Scotia smoked salmon are not really eating lox since real lox is not smoked, but cured in brine.

And while we are on the subject of pseudo-Jewish food, many round baked dough rings are not really bagels although they are sold as bagels.

Real bagels are boiled in water before baking, but many stores are merely steaming them instead of the authentic boiling before baking.

Insist on the real thing!

Cranberry Latkes Harriet H. Klayman ✳ Boylston, Massachusetts

12 ounces fresh cranberries	1 cup flour
¾ cup water	2 eggs
1½ cups golden raisins	canola oil
½ cup orange juice	whipped cream, if desired
2 cups sugar	

- In a large pot, simmer cranberries in water until they pop. Add raisins, orange juice, and sugar, mixing well. Boil until thickened.
- Remove from heat and let cool.
- Mix in flour and eggs.
- Heat canola oil in a skillet. Drop batter by tablespoonfuls into heated oil and fry until latkes are brown on both sides.
- Served with whipped cream on top, if desired.

Yield: 12 servings

The three braids on a challah symbolize truth, peace, and justice, and the white napkin that covers it represents the dew that collected on the manna in the morning during the long journey of the Israelites from Egypt to the Promised Land.

Croissant French Toast Sharyn Maxine Cohen ✳ Reading, Pennsylvania

margarine or cooking oil spray

4 croissants, split in half lengthwise

1 10-ounce jar orange marmalade

1½ ounces orange liqueur

1 teaspoon almond extract

1 cup regular or fat-free cream, or
 nondairy cream substitute

Egg Beaters equivalent to 4 eggs

- Grease a baking dish with margarine.
- Place bottom half of croissants side by side in baking dish. Set aside.
- Mix together orange marmalade and orange liqueur. Spread two thirds of marmalade mixture on croissants in baking dish. Cover with top half of croissants. Set aside.
- Mix together almond extract, cream, and Egg Beaters and pour over croissants. Spread remaining marmalade over top.
- Chill in refrigerator overnight.
- Preheat oven to 350° F.
- Bake for about 30 minutes, until eggs have set and top is crusty and browned.
- This French toast is great for "Breaking the fast."

Yield: 4 servings

Honey-Cinnamon Grits   Edith Carreker ∗ Atlanta, Georgia

2⅓ cups water

1 cup skim milk

⅔ cup hominy grits

½ teaspoon salt

2 tablespoons honey

1 teaspoon cinnamon

▪ Combine water and milk in a saucepan and heat to boiling. Slowly stir in hominy grits and return to a boil. Add salt.

▪ Reduce heat to a simmer and cover. Simmer for 25 to 30 minutes, stirring occasionally.

▪ Remove from heat and stir in honey and cinnamon.

Yield: 2 servings

Salt has a significant place in Jewish life.

The Talmud says that "The world can get along without pepper, but it cannot get along without salt." Treaties were sealed with salt and in Numbers 18:19 there is the "everlasting covenant of salt."

The mayor of Jerusalem often greets important visitors at the entrance to the city with an offering of bread and salt. Similarly, it is a Jewish tradition to bring bread and salt to people who have just moved into a new home.

Super Soups

Blender Borsht Lorraine P. Melworth * Richmond, Virginia

2 1-pound cans beets

1 12-ounce can frozen apple juice concentrate

⅔ to ¾ cup bottled lemon juice

1 tablespoon onion powder

1 teaspoon Mrs. Dash

sour cream or yogurt, if desired

- Place canned beets with liquid in blender and purée. Pour purée from blender into 4-quart pot. Fill one of the beet cans halfway with water and pour into emptied blender. Blend for a few seconds to rinse out blender and then pour water into pot with beets. Add apple juice concentrate, lemon juice, onion powder, and Mrs. Dash.
- Heat to boiling. Lower heat and simmer for 10 minutes.
- Garnish with a dollop of sour cream or yogurt.
- Soup can be served hot or cold. Borsht can be kept in refrigerator for 10 days to 2 weeks.

Yield: 8 servings

The maxim "An apple a day keeps the doctor away" has its basis in Jewish lore. In early Talmudic times, apples were believed to have medicinal value and they were sent to people in ill health.

Lentil Soup Daniel Dewberry * Atlanta, Georgia

1½ quarts chicken stock	salt, to taste
1 pound lentils	pepper, to taste
1 onion, sliced	3 tablespoons olive oil
2 cloves	3 garlic cloves
2 bay leaves	8 kosher hot dogs, sliced

- Place chicken stock in a heavy pan. Add lentils and heat to boiling. Lower heat to a simmer and add onion, cloves, bay leaves, salt, and pepper.
- Cover and let simmer for about 1 hour, until lentils are soft.
- Remove about 1½ cups of the lentils and drain liquid back into soup.
- Purée removed lentils in a food processor and then return to soup.
- Keep soup at a simmer.
- In a small pan, heat olive oil and sauté garlic cloves until almost golden brown.
- Remove garlic from pan and add to simmering soup.
- Put hot dog slices in pan and cook for 3 to 5 minutes. Pour oil and hot dogs into soup and cook soup for another 10 minutes.
- Remove from heat and let sit for 1 to 2 hours, then refrigerate overnight. Soup is tastier if served the day after it is made.

Yield: 8 servings

Easy Chicken Soup   Rachel Epperson * Chicago, Illinois

1 4- to 5-pound chicken, cut into pieces

3 quarts water

2 carrots, sliced

2 celery stalks, sliced

2 parsley sprigs

1 bay leaf

1 tablespoon salt

1 teaspoon pepper

- Place chicken pieces and water in a large pot, cover, and heat to a boil. Reduce heat to a simmer. Add carrots, celery, parsley, bay leaf, salt, and pepper.
- Simmer for about 3 hours.
- Remove from heat and strain broth into a large bowl. Remove bay leaf.
- Set aside chicken and vegetables to cool.
- Refrigerate strained broth.
- Remove chicken meat from skin and bones and discard skin and bones. Set aside.
- When broth has chilled, remove fat from top and then add chicken and vegetables. Reheat soup before serving.

Yield: 8 servings

Your mother and grandmother were right.

They said chicken soup—affectionately called "Jewish penicillin"—is good for a cold and if you eat some you will feel better.

And now there is scientific proof, 800 years after the twelfth-century rabbi and physician Maimonides wrote that "soup made from an old chicken is of benefit against chronic fevers" and that it "also aids the cough."

While any warm fluid will help relieve the symptoms of a cold, chicken soup is extra good at doing so, according to Dr. Margaret Gradison, whose field is family and community medicine at the Duke University Medical Center in North Carolina.

Dr. Gradison points out that chicken soup is "packed with protein, vitamins, and minerals, all of which can aid in the fight against cold germs."

But maybe you want a second opinion.

How about Dr. Bruce Krieger, a pulmonologist at Mount Sinai Medical Center in Miami, Florida. A study was done at that hospital to determine the most effective ways to clear up nasal congestion. A comparison was done between the benefits of sipping chicken soup, hot water, and cold water.

Chicken soup came out on top.

Simply stated by Dr. Krieger, "Chicken soup has a decongestant effect."

Besides the benefits of the warm fluid, Dr. Irwin Ziment, chief of medicine at Olive View–UCLA Medical Center and an expert in respiratory pharmacology, points out that cystine, an amino acid that is abundant in chicken, is chemically similar to a drug that is prescribed for bronchitis and other respiratory infections. That drug is acetylcysteine and it was originally made from chicken feathers and skin.

As good as plain chicken soup is to ease a cold, it can be made even more effective with the addition of hot, pungent ingredients. Things like garlic, hot peppers, horseradish, mustard, ginger, and curry powder break up congestion and flush out sinuses.

Sukkoth Soup   Deborah S. Lewitter ✳ Highland Park, New Jersey

approximately 1 pound flanken

3 large meaty marrow bones

*1 package fresh soup greens (such as car-
    rots, leeks, scallions, parsnip, turnip,
    parsley, and dill)*

*2 6-ounce packages kosher-style dried
    soup mixes, 1 noodle and 1 vegetable*

*1 1-pound package frozen soup vegeta-
    bles (these are thick-cut vegetables)*

▪ In a large pot, place flanken, marrow bones, and fresh soup greens. Add enough water to completely cover. Bring to a boil. Skim foam.

▪ Reduce heat and simmer for approximately 1½ hours.

▪ Remove flanken and continue simmering for an additional hour.

▪ Remove vegetables from soup.

▪ Purée carrots, parsnip, and turnip and return to soup. Discard leeks, scallions, parsley, and dill.

▪ Add dried soup mixes, reserving packages of spices. Cook soup according to directions on dried soup mix packages. Add frozen soup vegetables 30 minutes before dried soup mix is done.

▪ Just before soup is ready, add contents of packages of spices and mix well.

▪ Remove bones from pot and discard.

▪ Flanken can be returned to soup or served separately.

Yield: 6 to 8 servings

Green Pea and Barley Soup Elaine Katz Hoffman ∗ Berkeley Heights, New Jersey

2 large onions, peeled and diced

1 pound carrots, peeled and diced

1 whole garlic head, peeled and chopped

4 celery stalks, peeled and diced

⅓ cup canola oil

salt, to taste

pepper, to taste

marjoram, to taste

2 large bay leaves

1 pound green shelled peas, washed and drained

3 tablespoons powdered vegetable bouillon

2 large parsnips, peeled and cut into chunks

2 large parsley roots, peeled and cut into chunks

1 large celery knob, peeled and cut into chunks

½ cup barley, washed and drained

1 bunch Italian parsley

1 bunch fresh dill

▪ In a large soup pot, sauté onions, carrots, garlic, and celery in canola oil until onions and garlic are golden. Sprinkle salt, pepper, and marjoram over vegetables as they are sautéing. Add bay leaves. Add peas and powdered vegetable bouillon, stirring to coat vegetables. Add parsnips, parsley root, and celery knob. Add water to cover all ingredients by 3 inches.

▪ Cover pot and simmer over low heat for 1½ hours, stirring every 20 minutes.

▪ Add barley, parsley, and dill. Cover pot and simmer for an additional 45 to 60 minutes.

▪ Check level of water as soup is cooking, adding more if necessary, so that mixture has the consistency of a soup, not a stew.

Yield: 6 to 8 servings

Lizzie's Matzoh Balls Claire Elise Sterne Hack ✻ Chesterfield, Missouri

14 regular tea matzohs (try not to substitute)

3 cups chicken or turkey consommé or broth

2 large onions, finely chopped

3 tablespoons pareve margarine

12 eggs, beaten

1 tablespoon red pepper (minimum)

1 tablespoon black pepper (minimum)

1 tablespoon ginger (minimum)

salt, to taste (optional)

1 cup matzoh cake meal (try not to substitute)

pareve cooking spray or oil

beef stew or soup

- Break matzohs into a large bowl. Add enough broth to moisten well and mix. Drain excess liquid. Set aside.
- Melt margarine in a skillet and sauté onions until lightly browned. Add onions, eggs, red pepper, black pepper, ginger, and salt to matzoh, mixing thoroughly. Add ⅓ cup of matzoh cake meal and mix with hands. Add ¼ cup more matzoh cake meal, mix, and taste. (Adding all the matzoh cake meal at once usually results in lumps and poor consistency.) Add additional seasonings to taste. (The key to this recipe is lots of seasonings since matzoh balls require much seasoning. Do not be shy.)
- Spray or oil skillet (even nonstick skillets) and cook half of matzoh mixture on low heat, stirring constantly, until dry, approximately 5 minutes. (Be sure to cook the matzoh in two batches. Otherwise it is too moist or it burns.)
- Remove from heat and place cooked matzoh in a bowl. Set aside.
- Respray or re-oil skillet and cook remaining matzoh mixture.
- Add parsley to cooked matzoh as desired and mix well.
- Cover and refrigerate for at least 4 hours. Mixture will keep in refrigerator up to 1 week.

- Grease hands and roll matzoh mixture into golf-ball-size balls. Roll balls in remaining matzoh cake meal.
- Cook matzoh balls in boiling stew or soup for only 5 to 7 minutes before serving. Overcooking will dissolve them.
- Our tradition is to serve the matzoh balls in beef stew rather than chicken broth. It is wonderful.
- Prepare only as many matzoh balls as needed for the next meal. Recipe can be halved.

Yield: 75 to 100 matzoh balls

There's one in every family: someone who would eat everything on the table if given the chance.

Well, here's something for them: Ben's Annual Charity Matzoh Ball Eating contest sponsored by Ben's Kosher Delicatessen & Caterers in New York City.

The goal of the contest is to eat as many matzoh balls as possible in the allotted time: two minutes and fifty seconds in the semifinal round and five minutes and twenty-five seconds in the final round. There is an assortment of prizes, and the top finisher also gets the coveted matzoh ball eating trophy.

To ensure that the contest is conducted fairly, there are strict rules. For example:

* Each contestant begins with five matzoh balls in broth and gets additional matzoh balls after he or she finishes those five.
* Contestants may eat either standing or sitting, using hands, knife, fork, and/or spoon.

And, most important, contestants must retain all matzoh balls ingested for five minutes following the end signal.

Chickpea and Lentil Soup   Caroline Fink   ✳   Naperville, Illinois

3 to 4 stalks celery, peeled and finely
    chopped

1 to 2 onions, finely chopped

1 tablespoon olive oil

2 cups lentils

3½ quarts water

2 cups cooked and drained chickpeas

¾ cup fresh cilantro, finely chopped

½ teaspoon ground ginger

½ teaspoon cinnamon

½ teaspoon turmeric

¼ teaspoon salt

dash of pepper

4 ripe tomatoes, chopped

3 tablespoons fresh lemon juice

■   In a large pot, sauté celery and onions in oil for about 5 minutes. Add lentils and water.

■   Cover and cook over medium heat for 35 to 40 minutes.

■   Add chickpeas, cilantro, ginger, cinnamon, turmeric, salt, and pepper. Cook for 15 minutes more. Add tomatoes and lemon juice and cook for another 15 minutes.

Yield: 8 servings

Vegetarian Jewish Cabbage Soup Jan Dash * Framingham, Massachusetts

4 tablespoons butter

1 medium cabbage, shredded

2 medium onions, chopped

2 tablespoons flour

2 teaspoons salt

½ teaspoon pepper

5 cups water

3 cups tomato juice

2 tablespoons sugar

1 teaspoon caraway seeds

1 cup sour cream

▪ In a 2-quart pot, melt the butter. Add cabbage and onions and slowly cook for about 15 minutes, until soft. Add flour, salt, pepper, water, tomato juice, sugar, and caraway seeds.

▪ Cook uncovered on low heat for 1 hour.

▪ Serve hot with a dollop of sour cream for each bowl.

Yield: 6 to 8 servings

Russian Jews practice the "flaming tea" ceremony to celebrate the burning lights of Hanukkah. Everyone puts a lump of sugar on a spoon, pours brandy on it, sets it on fire, and then drops the burning lump of sugar into a glass of tea.

Chicken Fricassee Rena Hartman ∗ San Diego, California

3½ pounds chicken pieces

½ cup celery pieces

1 red pepper, chopped

1 mild onion, sliced

1 garlic clove, minced

2 bay leaves

½ teaspoon ground ginger

½ teaspoon paprika

salt, to taste

pepper, to taste

Fricassee Sauce (recipe follows)

- Place chicken pieces, celery, pepper, onion, garlic, bay leaves, ginger, paprika, salt, and pepper in a large pot.
- Cover with boiling water and simmer with a lid on the pot until chicken is tender, about 3 hours.
- Remove from heat, drain, and remove bay leaves.
- Serve with fricassee sauce.

Yield: 6 to 8 servings

Fricassee Sauce

½ cup chicken fat

¼ cup flour

1½ to 2 cups hot chicken stock

1 teaspoon salt

dash of pepper

½ cup warm nondairy creamer

- Heat chicken fat and slowly add flour, chicken stock, salt, and pepper. Mix in nondairy creamer, stirring until smooth.

Black-Eyed Peas and Lamb Stew   Stella Rittman * Pittsburgh, Pennsylvania

1 pound dried black-eyed peas, soaked in
    water for at least 1 hour

2 onions, chopped

2 to 3 tablespoons vegetable oil

3 garlic cloves, minced

3 pounds lamb, cut into small pieces

3 large tomatoes, cut into small pieces

¼ cup tomato paste

¾ teaspoon cinnamon

¼ teaspoon allspice

¼ teaspoon mint

½ teaspoon salt

¼ teaspoon freshly ground pepper

1 tablespoon sugar

- Drain black-eyed peas, place in a pot, cover with water, and simmer for about 20 minutes. Set aside.
- Sauté onions in vegetable oil in a large frying pan until golden. Add garlic and cook for 1 to 2 minutes, then add lamb pieces. Cook until lamb pieces are browned. Add tomato pieces and tomato paste. Add cooked black-eyed peas. Add cinnamon, allspice, mint, salt, and pepper.
- Cook for 1 hour.
- Add sugar, stirring well.
- Cook for another hour, or until lamb is tender.

Yield: 6 servings

Chicken Couscous Michelle Ordynans ✳ West Nyack, New York

1 tablespoon oil

2 to 3 garlic cloves, minced

1 small onion, diced

2 to 3 pounds chicken parts, skin removed

1 cup couscous (millet may be substituted)

3 cups water

1 red bell pepper, thinly sliced

½ teaspoon cumin

1 teaspoon salt

a few drops of hot pepper sauce, optional

■ Heat oil in a skillet. Add garlic and onion. Cook for 2 to 3 minutes. Add chicken parts, couscous, water, bell pepper, cumin, salt, and hot pepper sauce, if desired.

■ Cover skillet and cook on low heat on top of stove for 45 to 60 minutes. Check occasionally and add more water as needed.

Yield: 4 to 6 servings

Garlic has been a popular food in the Middle East for a long, long time.

It is mentioned in Numbers 11:5 as one of the foods the Israelites ate in Egypt during their bondage, and what they yearned for during their long years wandering in the wilderness.

Early Jews believed that garlic possessed aphrodisiac qualities and, according to a tradition mentioned in the Jerusalem Talmud, Ezra decreed that garlic be eaten on Friday evenings because it "promotes and arouses sexual desire."

Pirogen   Andrea Stein * Los Angeles, California

Filling

1 onion, sliced

chicken fat for frying

2 pounds cooked beef

½ teaspoon onion salt

Pastry Shell

¼ pound margarine

¼ cup oil

2 eggs

⅓ cup water

2 cups flour

1½ teaspoons baking powder

1 teaspoon sugar

½ teaspoon baking soda

¼ teaspoon salt

- For the filling, fry onion in chicken fat. Grind together dried onion and cooked beef. Mix in onion salt.
- Divide into 24 portions.
- For the pastry, mix together margarine, oil, eggs, water, flour, baking powder, sugar, baking soda, and salt until well blended.
- Knead on floured surface. Roll out dough and cut into 24 squares.
- Preheat oven to 375° F. Grease a cookie sheet.
- Place one portion of filling in the center of each pastry shell.
- Fold corners of pastry shells crosswise to form triangles. Press edges together firmly with a fork dipped in flour and then place on cookie sheet.
- Bake for about 20 minutes, until brown.

Yield: 4 servings

Lemon Chicken Judy Lawrence ✳ Aurora, Colorado

4 chicken breasts

Soy-Sesame Marinade (recipe follows)

2 tablespoons corn muffin mix

1 egg, beaten

vegetable oil for frying

4 lemon slices

Lemon Sauce (recipe follows)

- Marinate chicken breasts in soy-sesame marinade for 1 to 2 hours.
- Combine corn muffin mix and egg and coat chicken breasts.
- Fry chicken breasts in vegetable oil, about 5 minutes on each side. Drain and garnish each breast with a lemon slice.
- Serve with lemon sauce.

Yield: 4 servings

Soy-Sesame Marinade

1½ tablespoons sugar

1½ tablespoons soy sauce

1½ tablespoons red or white wine

1 teaspoon sesame oil

1 teaspoon salt

dash of pepper

- Combine sugar, soy sauce, wine, sesame oil, salt, and pepper, mixing together well.

Lemon Sauce

¼ cup lemon juice

3 tablespoons sugar

2 tablespoons corn muffin mix

1½ tablespoons cornstarch

1 cup water

1 tablespoon oil

½ teaspoon salt

2 egg yolks

▪ Mix together lemon juice, sugar, corn muffin mix, cornstarch, water, oil, and salt. Add egg yolks and heat, stirring, for 5 minutes.

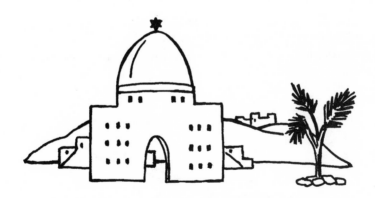

Shabbos Buffet Tabbouli
Beverly Koronet ✴ River Vale, New Jersey

2 cups chicken broth

1 cup bulgur

⅓ cup olive oil or other salad oil

¼ cup fresh lemon juice

1½ teaspoons salt

¾ teaspoon ground allspice

2 tablespoons chopped fresh mint

1 bunch scallions, finely chopped (white and green parts)

1½ cups packed parsley, finely chopped

2 medium tomatoes, finely diced

lettuce leaves, hollowed-out tomatoes, or hollowed-out green pepper shells

▪ Bring chicken broth to a boil. Pour over bulgur and let stand for 2 hours, stirring occasionally, until broth is absorbed by bulgur.

▪ Mix in well olive oil, lemon juice, salt, allspice, mint, scallions, parsley, and tomatoes.

▪ Chill in refrigerator for several hours or overnight.

▪ Serve on lettuce leaves, in hollowed-out tomatoes, or in hollowed-out green pepper shells.

Yield: 6 to 8 servings

Leftover Chicken Casserole Hallie Kaufman ✳ Sausalito, California

3 cups cooked noodles

1 cup seasoned bread crumbs

3 cups cooked chicken pieces without bones

1 cup sliced portobello mushrooms

¼ cup minced onion

1 garlic clove, minced

2 tablespoons chopped fresh parsley

dash of salt

2 cups chicken stock

2 tablespoons vegetable oil

- Preheat oven to 350° F.
- Layer noodles in a greased casserole dish. Sprinkle with ¼ cup of the bread crumbs. Layer chicken pieces and sprinkle with ¼ cup of the bread crumbs. Layer mushrooms on top and then sprinkle with onion, garlic, parsley, salt, and remaining ½ cup of bread crumbs.
- Gently pour chicken stock around edges of dish. Sprinkle vegetable oil over top.
- Bake for 30 to 40 minutes, until top is brown.

Yield: 4 to 6 servings

American-style bagels are popular not only here in the United States.
Korcarz, a kosher bakery and restaurant run by Michael Korcarz on the Rue des Rosiers in the Jewish section of Le Marais in Paris, provides bagels to Euro Disney and the United States Army in Europe.

Fruit and Potato Casserole Dianne Boykin * Alexandria, Virginia

¾ cup dried apricots

½ cup prunes, pitted

¼ cup raisins

2 cups boiling water

3 tablespoons margarine, melted

1½ pounds sweet potatoes, skins washed
well, cut into ¼-inch to ½-inch slices

salt, to taste

pepper, to taste

1½ pounds white potatoes, skins washed
well, cut into ½-inch-thick slices

Honey Glaze (recipe follows)

■ Place apricots, prunes, and raisins in a bowl and pour boiling water over them. Let soak for about 30 minutes. Drain.

■ Preheat oven to 400° F.

■ Pour melted margarine into a 2-quart baking dish and place sweet potato slices in dish. Sprinkle salt and pepper over top.

■ Bake for 20 to 30 minutes, stirring once or twice, until potatoes are tender.

■ Place white potato slices in a saucepan and cover with water. Heat to boiling, then cover pan and simmer over low heat for about 15 minutes, until potatoes are tender. Remove from heat and drain.

■ Gently fold white potato slices into sweet potato and fruit mixture in baking pan.

■ Pour honey glaze over top.

■ Bake for 15 minutes, stirring several times to coat evenly.

■ Remove from oven and gently stir to mix completely.

■ Return to oven and bake for 15 minutes more.

Yield: 4 to 6 servings

Honey Glaze

½ cup honey

3 tablespoons margarine

½ cup apple juice

½ teaspoon ground cinnamon

pinch of ground cloves

■ Combine honey, margarine, apple juice, cinnamon, and cloves in a small saucepan and heat to a simmer.

Each year about 2 million airline passengers order an estimated 2½ million kosher meals on flights within the United States and flights originating in this country.

Experts who are involved in the airline kosher food industry say the percentage of kosher meals that is ordered by non-Jews ranges from a low of 30 percent up to a high of 50 percent.

The amount that airlines pay for the kosher meals they serve goes from $1.25 for a snack all the way up to over $12 for a meal in the first class section on an international flight.

The average cost, though, is $2.50 for the chicken dish that is the most commonly served kosher meal.

Salmon Loaf Louis Isaacson ✳ Berkeley, California

2 cups bread crumbs

½ cup milk

2 14.75-ounce cans salmon

1 egg, beaten

½ teaspoon salt

2 teaspoons minced fresh parsley

1 teaspoon tarragon flakes

2 tablespoons margarine, melted

1 tablespoon fresh lemon juice

- Preheat oven to 375° F. Grease a baking dish.
- Soften bread crumbs in milk. Set aside.
- Drain salmon and remove skin. Bones may be left in. Place in a large bowl and add softened bread crumbs, egg, salt, parsley, tarragon, margarine, and lemon juice. Mix together well.
- Spoon salmon mixture into baking dish, patting down firmly.
- Fill a larger pan with hot water and place the salmon pan into it.
- Bake for 40 to 50 minutes, until loaf is firm.

Yield: 6 servings

Verenikas Rivka Pollard * Los Angeles, California

2 cups mashed potatoes

¼ cup matzoh cake meal

½ teaspoon salt

dash of pepper

3 eggs, beaten

1 cup chopped cooked brisket

½ cup matzoh meal

vegetable oil or chicken fat for frying

- Mix together potatoes, matzoh cake meal, salt, pepper, and 2 of the eggs. Form into balls.
- Using your thumb, form a hole in each of the balls. Fill holes with chopped meat and enclose potato ball entirely around meat.
- Dip potato balls in remaining egg and then roll balls in matzoh meal.
- Fry balls in vegetable oil or chicken fat. Turn only once to brown both sides.

Yield: 4 servings

The culinary variety of foods available in the supermarket that are certified kosher just keeps growing and growing.

For example, Floribbean is a company founded by Margarita Ross, a non-Jewish immigrant from Nicaragua. Among the products offered by Floribbean that carry the Ⓤ certification are Key Lime Calypso Dip; Passionhot Pepper Jelly; Papaya Chutney with Rum; Green Mango Jelly; and Goomboy Mango, Ginger, and Key Lime Barbeque Sauce.

Pineapple Soy Chicken   Adam Singer ✳ Santa Monica, California

½ to ¾ cup flour

½ teaspoon salt

2 1½-pound chickens, cut into halves

vegetable oil for frying

1 cup grated fresh pineapple

1 tomato, sliced

1 green pepper, sliced

1 tablespoon soy sauce

¾ cup sliced almonds

4 sprigs fresh parsley

- Mix together flour and salt. Dredge chicken halves in flour and salt mixture.
- Cook chicken halves in oil until done.
- Remove from pan and set aside on a serving platter or individual dishes.
- Combine pineapple, tomato, and green pepper and add to hot oil in pan. Add soy sauce and carefully stir together. Cook until heated and then pour over chicken.
- Sprinkle chicken with almonds and garnish with parsley sprigs.

Yield: 4 servings

Tuna and Rice Salad Linda Martin ✳ Tempe, Arizona

4 cups cooked rice

*2 6-ounce cans tuna in oil, drained and
 flaked*

½ cup chopped green pepper

½ cup chopped red pepper

¼ cup balsamic vinegar

1 teaspoon Dijon mustard

1 teaspoon sugar

2 hard-boiled eggs, chopped

2 teaspoons chopped fresh chives

■ Mix together rice and tuna in a large bowl. Add green pepper, red pepper, vinegar, mustard, and sugar. Mix well. Add eggs and chives and mix together again.

Yield: 4 servings

Although no longer in business, Lou G. Segal's, the popular landmark kosher restaurant in the garment district in Manhattan, did more than just feed the Jewish workers in that area.

The restaurant provided most of the kosher meals that were served by airlines to its Orthodox passengers fifty years ago.

Lou G. Segal's was soon displaced by Schrieber's, a Brooklyn company that employed many Jewish immigrants and introduced frozen kosher meals that could be delivered and served anywhere in the world.

Onion Cheese Pie Gloria Forman * Indianapolis, Indiana

3 Vidalia or sweet onions, thinly sliced

2 tablespoons sweet margarine

2 eggs

½ cup nonfat milk

2 tablespoons flour

¼ teaspoon salt

½ cup shredded Cheddar or Jarlsberg
   cheese

- Preheat oven to 375° F. Grease an 8- or 9-inch pie plate.
- In a heavy pan, sauté onions in margarine for about 10 minutes, until soft. Remove from heat and set aside.
- Mix together eggs, milk, flour, and salt. Add sautéed onions.
- Pour onion mixture into pie plate. Sprinkle cheese over top.
- Bake for about 20 minutes, until cheese is browned.

Yield: 4 to 6 servings

As of April, 1999, twenty states, including New York, New Jersey, Connecticut, Pennsylvania, Ohio, and California, have comprehensive kosher laws on their books regulating, among other things, how foods must conform to kashrus laws, how kosher foods must be displayed and labeled, and how kosher foods must be kept separate from nonkosher foods.

There is a growing movement to have federal legislation passed by Congress to standardize kosher rules and regulations so consumers will have the assurance of getting certified kosher foods no matter where they shop in the United States.

Sally's Sweet and Sour Meatballs Iris Seidman ✳ Somerset, New Jersey

1 10-¾-ounce can tomato soup

½ cup brown sugar

¼ cup lemon juice

½ cup water

2 small onions, diced

1 egg

milk (to make recipe kosher, use a
      nondairy substitute such as soy milk
      or rice milk)

1 pound chopped meat

▪ Combine tomato soup, brown sugar, lemon juice, water, and onions in a large pot and heat to boiling.

▪ Combine egg and enough milk to make ¾ cup. Mix well with chopped meat. Form into small meatballs.

▪ Drop meatballs into boiling soup mixture, cover, and let simmer over low heat for about 1 hour.

Yield: 4 servings

Chicken à la King David
Harriet Eddleman ✳ Denver, Colorado

1 cup sliced portobello mushrooms
1 tablespoon vegetable oil
¼ cup chicken fat
¼ cup flour
2 cups chicken stock

3 cups diced cooked chicken
⅓ cup pimiento, chopped
2 egg yolks
½ teaspoon salt
¼ teaspoon pepper

- Sauté mushrooms in vegetable oil. Set aside.
- Heat chicken fat in a large heavy pan. Blend in flour and slowly add chicken stock. When sauce is smooth and bubbling, add chicken pieces, mushrooms, and pimiento.
- Reduce heat and stir in egg yolks. Add salt and pepper, stirring until sauce has thickened.

Yield: 4 to 6 servings

How much do Jewish people value food? Consider this. Ron Rosenbaum, a columnist for *The New York Observer*, described the chopped liver served at Barney Greengrass on Amsterdam Avenue, a restaurant that has been around since 1906, as "one of the supreme achievements of Jewish-American civilization."

And Gary Greengrass, the grandson of the restaurant's founder, declared, "I'm in the entertainment business. Food is theater, food is sexy. Food is, you know, all those adjectives out there."

Sweet and Sour Brisket of Beef   Sandi Finkelstein ✳ San Francisco, California

2 pounds brisket of beef

2 onions, sliced

1 bay leaf

3 tablespoons sugar

3 tablespoons apple cider vinegar

¾ cup boiling water

½ cup white raisins

½ teaspoon salt

¼ teaspoon pepper

- Place brisket in a heavy pot. Add onions, bay leaf, sugar, vinegar, water, raisins, salt, and pepper.
- Cover and simmer for about 3 hours, until meat is tender.
- Remove bay leaf before serving.

Yield: 4 servings

Why is corned beef called "corned beef" if no corn is used making it?

The name comes from the corn-kernel-sized granules of dry salt that is used to make it. Indeed, in London our corned beef is called "salt beef" and in the rest of England it is known as "pickled beef."

Sauerbraten Lenore Pennella ✴ Stamford, Connecticut

1½ cups red wine

2 tablespoons minced onion

2 garlic cloves, minced

1 tablespoon brown sugar

dash of thyme

3½ to 4 pounds boneless chuck

1 bay leaf

½ cup flour

½ teaspoon salt

1 cup boiling water

- Combine wine, onion, garlic, brown sugar, and thyme.
- Place meat in a deep pot and pour wine mixture over it. Add bay leaf.
- Cover and refrigerate for 6 hours or overnight.
- Preheat oven to 450° F.
- Remove meat from marinade and blot dry. Reserve marinade.
- Mix together flour and salt and sprinkle onto meat.
- Place meat uncovered in a roasting pan and bake until meat begins to brown, 20 to 30 minutes.
- Add boiling water and reserved marinade, cover, reduce heat to 350° F, and cook, with occasional basting, until meat is tender, about 3 hours.
- Remove bay leaf before serving.

Yield: 6 servings

My Mother's Chicken Stew Fred Brisendine * Marietta, Georgia

3 pounds chicken, cut into pieces

1 teaspoon salt

1 teaspoon tarragon

pepper, to taste

¼ cup olive oil

1½ cups diced onions

½ cup boiling water

2 cups tomato sauce

- Sprinkle chicken pieces with salt, tarragon, and pepper. Set aside.
- Put olive oil in a heavy skillet and heat. When oil is hot, carefully place chicken pieces in oil and brown on all sides. Add onions and continue cooking until onions are tender and light brown. Add water and cover.
- Simmer for about 15 minutes and then add tomato sauce, simmering for another 15 to 20 minutes, until chicken is tender.

Yield: 4 to 6 servings

The Jewish fondness for eating was well known even back in the thirteenth century. French Jews were criticized at that time for "studying the Talmud with their stomachs full of meat, vegetables, and wine."

Gingersnap Burgers Paula Snyder ✳ New Haven, Connecticut

2 pounds lean ground beef

2 onions, finely chopped

1 egg, beaten

½ cup seasoned bread crumbs

dash of salt

dash of pepper

2 tablespoons vegetable oil

1 cup tomato sauce

1 cup water

¼ cup apple cider vinegar

½ cup brown sugar

6 whole cloves

10 to 12 gingersnap cookies, finely
  crumbled

- Combine beef, onions, egg, bread crumbs, salt, and pepper.
- Form into 8 patties.
- Fry in vegetable oil in a heavy skillet until brown on one side.
- While frying, mix together tomato sauce, water, vinegar, brown sugar, cloves, and gingersnaps.
- Turn burgers in pan and slowly pour gingersnap mixture over patties. Bring to a slow boil, reduce heat to a simmer, and simmer until meat is cooked and sauce has thickened.

Yield: 8 servings

Apricot-Coconut Glazed Chicken
Karen Abramson * Silver Spring, Maryland

1 8-ounce bottle French salad dressing

1 1.2-ounce package onion soup mix

1 cup apricot preserves

½ cup flaked coconut

½ cup orange juice

4 to 6 large chicken breasts, skin and bones removed, cut into bite-size pieces

- Preheat oven to 325° F.
- Mix together salad dressing, onion soup mix, apricot preserves, coconut, and orange juice. Stir in chicken pieces.
- Pour into a 9 x 13-inch baking pan.
- Bake for 1¼ to 1½ hours until done. Stir once or twice while baking.

Yield: 4 to 6 servings

There is progress, and there is *progress*.

Oreo cookies, which once contained lard, are now certified kosher and carry the Ⓤ symbol.

And, by the way, M&Ms are kosher, as is Coors beer (the first major beer to be certified kosher), Budweiser, and Coca-Cola.

One-Pot Sauerbraten Monica Ziegler * Lakewood, Colorado

4 pounds pot roast
½ teaspoon salt
1 cup wine vinegar
1 cup boiling water
1 large onion, thinly sliced
2 bay leaves

10 whole cloves
6 whole peppercorns
2 tablespoons sugar
3 tablespoons vegetable oil
6 gingersnap cookies, finely crumbled

▪ Place meat in a large pot. Sprinkle with salt and pour vinegar and boiling water over top. Add onion, bay leaves, cloves, peppercorns, and sugar. Stir together.

▪ Refrigerate for 24 to 36 hours, turning meat often.

▪ Remove meat and pat dry. Reserve marinade.

▪ Brown meat on all sides in vegetable oil. Place meat in a Crock-Pot, pour reserved marinade over top, cover, and cook for 7 to 8 hours, until done.

▪ Remove meat, strain juices discarding the solids, and add gingersnaps to strained juice to thicken, stirring well.

▪ Serve meat with gingersnap sauce.

Yield: 4 to 6 servings

Patty's Mushroom Patties Patty Margolis * Washington, D.C.

3 cups brown rice

1 cup orange juice

1 pound mushrooms, finely chopped

¼ cup flour

¼ teaspoon salt

¼ teaspoon pepper

vegetable oil for frying

- Cook brown rice according to package directions, substituting 1 cup orange juice for 1 cup of the water. Remove from heat.
- Stir in mushrooms, flour, salt, and pepper.
- Using a processor or a blender, mix until rice can be formed into patties.
- Form into 12 patties.
- Place patties in a heavy skillet and fry in vegetable oil for about 8 to 12 minutes on each side to desired doneness.

Servings: 6 servings

While the Orthodox Union is the dominant kosher food certification agency with its nearly ubiquitous Ⓤ, a survey by *Kashrus Magazine* found 345 different national or regional kosher certification symbols on food products sold in the United States.

Tomato-Mushroom Sauce
Jane Zafrin Shane ✳ Neshanic Station, New Jersey

1 large celery stalk, cut into small pieces
1 small onion, chopped
1 green pepper, chopped

1½ pounds mushrooms, sliced
1 46-ounce can tomato juice

- Place celery, onion, green pepper, mushrooms, and tomato juice in a skillet.
- Cook on low heat for 1 hour. This can be served with a number of dishes—rice, meat, chicken, pasta, you name it!

Yield: approximately 6 cups sauce

Time, geography, and new generations are making their mark on traditional Jewish foods.

Leonard Rubin grew up eating typical Eastern European foods at the family Seders. He would have gefilte fish, matzoh ball soup, sweet potato tzimmes, and brisket. When he became chef at the Phoenician Resort in Scottsdale, Arizona, and immersed himself in the Southwestern cuisine that relies greatly on chili, he made some changes.

He made gefilte fish with talapia instead of carp and served it with salsa instead of beets and horseradish. Chicken lime soup is home to his matzoh balls and Anaheim chilies hold his tzimmes. Mr. Rubin's brisket is blackened with fourteen different spices.

Michael Schuchat grew up in Baltimore where, bending to that city's fascination with crabs and shrimp, he started using Old Bay seasonings on his gefilte fish.

Locally popular fish have replaced the traditional carp, whitefish, and pike in various dishes. In the Pacific Northwest cooks use salmon; in Maine, haddock is preferred; red snapper is the choice in Florida; catfish is used in Louisiana.

Homemade matzoh balls have not escaped change either. Pecans are added to matzoh balls in Texas, while in Baton Rouge a spicier version is made with scallions and black pepper. The typical "Yankee matzoh ball' is scorned in Louisiana as being too big, too bland, and too mushy.

Grandma Lena's Stuffed Cabbage
Mara R. Kupperman ✳ New Orleans, Louisiana

The Cabbage

2 cabbages

2 pounds ground meat

2 eggs

¾ cup uncooked rice

salt, to taste

pepper, to taste

The Sauce

1 large onion, sliced

2 tablespoons margarine

2 15-ounce cans tomato sauce

1 quart water

3 tablespoons lemon juice

¼ cup brown sugar

⅓ cup ketchup

3 carrots, chopped

3 celery stalks, chopped

1 1-pound can whole berry cranberry
    sauce

1 cup raisins

½ cup prunes, if desired

salt, to taste

pepper, to taste

- Several days in advance of making recipe, place the cabbages in freezer.
- One day in advance, remove cabbages from freezer and defrost. Cabbage leaves will be limp and ready to use. Separate leaves, wash, and pat dry. Set aside.
- Combine ground meat, eggs, uncooked rice, salt, and pepper, mixing thoroughly.
- Form into meatballs.
- Fill cabbage leaves with meatballs. Roll and tuck in all sides of leaves.
- For the sauce, sauté onion in margarine.

- Put tomato sauce and water in a deep pot and bring to a boil. Add onion, lemon juice, brown sugar, ketchup, carrots, celery, cranberry sauce, raisins, prunes, salt, and pepper.
- Simmer over low heat.
- Put stuffed cabbage leaves in sauce, cover, and simmer for 2 hours.

Yield: 8 to 10 servings

A survey by the Food Science Center at Cornell University found that 61 percent of all the products on supermarket shelves are certified kosher. (This certification is known as a "Hechsher.")

The survey included stores in Ithaca, New York, where Cornell is located, as well as stores in New York City, Baltimore, and even Salina, Kansas.

Of the approximately 30,000 supermarkets in the United States, about 5,000 of them have a kosher food section.

The preference for kosher foods goes beyond just observant Jews. Muslims look for the kosher label because of the similarity between kosher rules and Islamic food laws called "hallal," or clean.

People who are lactose intolerant or who eschew all dairy foods choose foods labeled "kosher nondairy" or "pareve," which means neutral, containing neither meat nor dairy products.

Many people who are not Jewish or Muslim buy kosher foods because they believe that it is healthier, cleaner, and prepared to higher standards than just the minimums that the government requires.

Eat Your Veggies

Shabbat Dinner Carrot Pudding
Karen Moskovitz Shagrin ✳ Youngstown, Ohio

12 tablespoons margarine, softened

1 cup brown sugar

1 egg

1½ cups grated carrots

juice of ½ lemon

1 cup flour

1 teaspoon baking powder

1 teaspoon baking soda dissolved in
1 tablespoon hot water

- Preheat oven to 350° F. Grease a 9-inch square baking pan or a mold.
- Cream margarine. Add brown sugar, egg, carrots, lemon juice, flour, baking powder, and hot water with dissolved baking soda. Mix together well.
- Put pudding in greased baking pan or mold.
- Bake for 30 to 35 minutes.
- Remove from oven and let cool a little before removing from baking pan.

Yield: 8 to 10 servings

Pomegranates are eaten at Rosh Hashanah because they are mentioned in the Torah as a fruit of the Land of Israel and because they are said to have 613 seeds, the same number as the number of commandments—the foundation for all Jewish laws—described in the Torah.

Sweet Potato Casserole Ann Borchardt ✳ Kansas City, Missouri

4 large sweet potatoes, cooked
¼ pound margarine, softened
1 teaspoon salt

½ teaspoon cinnamon
½ cup brown sugar
2 cups mini-marshmallows

- Preheat oven to 350° F.
- Peel and mash the sweet potatoes. Mix in margarine, salt, and cinnamon. Stir in brown sugar.
- Place potatoes in a 2-quart casserole dish.
- Bake for 20 minutes.
- Remove from oven and sprinkle mini-marshmallows evenly over top of potatoes.
- Return to oven and bake for another 10 minutes, until mini-marshmallows are golden brown.

Yield: 4 servings

Coleslaw and Radish Salad   Nina Insley * Baltimore, Maryland

1 large red cabbage, grated (remove core
    first)
1 large carrot, grated
4 radishes, grated
1 small mild onion, grated
¼ cup plus 1 tablespoon apple cider
    vinegar

2 tablespoons sugar
¼ cup plus 2 tablespoons olive oil
1 teaspoon brown mustard
salt, to taste
pepper, to taste

- Mix together cabbage, carrot, radishes, and onion. Stir in vinegar, sugar, olive oil, mustard, salt, and pepper, mixing well.
- Refrigerate before serving.

Yield: 6 servings

When a list is made of the contributions by Jewish immigrants from Germany to the United States, perhaps at the top of the list should be the beef sausage–the hot dog–served in a soft bun.

Eggplant Salad   Ruth Kessler   *   Rockville, Maryland

4 medium eggplants

2 teaspoons minced fresh garlic

3 tablespoons minced onion

¼ cup mayonnaise

1 tablespoon fresh lemon juice

dash of salt

dash of pepper

dash of paprika

1 cup sliced black olives

- Preheat oven to 400° F.
- Pierce eggplants several times with a fork.
- Place whole eggplants on a greased cookie sheet.
- Bake for 30 minutes. Turn over eggplants and bake for another 30 to 40 minutes, until eggplants are soft.
- Remove from oven and let cool.
- Peel skins from eggplants and then blot with paper towels. Cut off tops and chop eggplants into small pieces. Eggplant will be partly puréed.
- In a large bowl, combine eggplant, garlic, onion, mayonnaise, lemon juice, salt, pepper, and paprika. Mix together well.
- Refrigerate until chilled.
- Garnish with black olives before serving.

Yield: 8 to 10 servings

Baked Carrot Casserole   Janice Reinhardt ✳ College Park, Maryland

2 pounds carrots, peeled and cut into ¼-
to ½-inch rounds

2 cups orange juice

1 small onion, finely chopped

1 tablespoon honey

1 teaspoon cinnamon

- Preheat oven to 375° F. Grease a casserole dish.
- Mix together carrots, orange juice, onion, honey, and cinnamon.
- Place carrot mixture in casserole dish and cover.
- Bake for about 1½ hours, until carrots are tender.

Yield: 6 servings

Even in times of stress and turmoil, Jews think about food.

Isaac Gomez was a well-connected Jewish man who lived in Spain during the Inquisition. Because he was a good friend of King Philip IV, the King set up a code to warn Gomez if the authorities were going to arrest him.

Gomez knew it was time to leave if the King sent him this special coded message: "The onions begin to smell."

Sweet Potato Special Elizabeth Fredericks ✳ Evanston, Illinois

6 baked sweet potatoes

¼ cup milk, heated

3 tablespoons margarine, softened

grated rind of 1 orange

juice of 1 orange

3 cups mini-marshmallows

- Preheat oven to 325° F.
- Cut potatoes in half lengthwise and remove insides. Mash potatoes with milk, margarine, orange rind, and juice.
- Return to potato skins.
- Sprinkle with mini-marshmallows.
- Bake for 25 to 30 minutes, until potatoes are hot and mini-marshmallows are melted and browned.

Yield: 6 servings

Great Grandpa Nathan's
"Salutée" Relish Evelyn Newfield * Jacksonville, Florida

1 1½- to 2-pound eggplant

6 jalepeño peppers

2 large cucumbers

½ cup apple cider vinegar

¼ cup sugar

½ teaspoon salt

½ teaspoon turmeric

- Peel the eggplant and cut into 1-inch-thick slices. Microwave on High for 10 minutes, until eggplant becomes soft. Squeeze out moisture from eggplant and set aside.
- Remove stems from peppers and then slit in two. Do not remove seeds. Microwave peppers on High for 45 seconds. Set aside.
- Peel cucumbers and cut into chunks.
- Coarsely grind the eggplant, peppers with the seeds, and cucumbers. Add vinegar, sugar, salt, and turmeric. Mix together well.
- Refrigerate relish for several days to mellow. It will keep in refrigerator for weeks.

Yield: 2 to 3 cups relish

Vegetable Medley Stacy Gaither ✳ Bloomington, Indiana

2 large carrots, peeled and sliced

1 small broccoli, chopped

1 large zucchini, sliced

1 cup apple juice

1 teaspoon caraway seeds

1 tablespoon margarine

½ cup slivered almonds

- Put carrots, broccoli, zucchini, apple juice, caraway seeds, and margarine in a large pot. Cover and heat to boiling. Reduce heat immediately and let simmer for 20 minutes.
- Arrange vegetables on a platter and sprinkle almonds over top before serving.

Yield: 4 servings

The bialy gets its name from the city of Bialystok, Poland, where it originated. The bialies here in America are a small version of the flat onion bread popular in Eastern Europe whose complete name is "Bialy stoker tsibele pletzel."

Palushki
(Polish Potato Dumplings) Gerda Seifer, née Krebs * Long Beach, California

6 to 8 large baking potatoes, cooked,
   drained, well mashed, and cooled

1 large egg

1 to 2 cups flour

salt, to taste

butter, heated until browned

- Combine potatoes, egg, and flour. Mix well. The amount of flour needed depends upon how absorbent the potatoes are. The dough should be smooth and not crumbly.
- Divide dough into four pieces. Using your hands, roll each piece into a ¾-inch-diameter log. Cut logs into 1½-inch pieces. The pieces will look like little fingers (palushki). Set aside.
- Bring a large pot of water to a fast boil. Add salt. Gently lay the dumplings into the pot. Stir with a long spoon and allow the dumplings to come up to the top. Boil the dumplings for 1 minute.
- Remove dumplings with a slotted spoon and place in a single layer on a flat dish or a bread board to dry.
- Repeat until all the dumplings have cooked.
- Work quickly since potato dough tends to thin out. If dough thins out, add more flour.
- After dumplings have dried and they will not stick together, place in a bowl and pour browned butter over top.
- Can be served with fried chopped onions or with pot roast and gravy.
- Dumplings can be fried the next day or frozen for another day.

Yield: 4 to 6 servings

Mashed Potato Cheese Puffs   Lorraine Gardner ✳ Highland Park, Illinois

3 cups hot mashed potatoes

1 teaspoon chopped chives

dash of pepper

2 tablespoons margarine

¾ cup grated Cheddar cheese

½ cup heavy cream, whipped

- Preheat oven to 350° F. Grease 4 oven cups.
- Mix together mashed potatoes, chives, pepper, and margarine. Divide into 4 portions and place into oven cups. Set aside.
- Add grated cheese to whipped cream and spread over potatoes.
- Bake for 15 minutes, or until nicely browned.

Yield: 4 servings

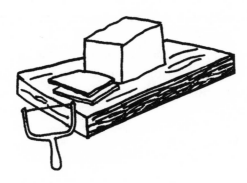

Bow Tie Noodles with Broccoli
and Bean Tomato Sauce Sheila G. Cohen * Lancaster, Pennsylvania

1 medium onion, peeled and chopped

1 garlic clove, minced

½ cup chicken or vegetable broth

3 tomatoes, diced, or 1 1-pound can low-
    salt stewed tomatoes

½ teaspoon salt

2 tablespoons oregano

¼ teaspoon pepper

½ pound mushrooms, thinly sliced

½ cup navy beans

½ cup broccoli florets

1 red pepper, seeded and chopped

2 carrots, thinly sliced

8 ounces bow tie noodles

- In a large skillet, combine onion, garlic, and chicken broth. Heat to boiling, reduce to a simmer and cook, stirring frequently, for about 5 minutes, until onion is soft. Stir in tomatoes, salt, oregano, and pepper and bring to a boil.

- Reduce to a simmer, cover, and cook, stirring occasionally, for about 15 minutes, until mixture is slightly thickened. Stir in mushrooms, navy beans, broccoli, red pepper, and carrots.

- Cover and cook for another 10 minutes, until vegetables are tender.

- While sauce is cooking, in a separate pot boil noodles according to package directions. Drain well, combine with sauce, and mix well.

Yield: 4 servings

Potato Latkes   Cecilia Byers ✳ St. Louis, Missouri

2 cups grated and drained potatoes

2 eggs, beaten

1¼ teaspoons salt

1 heaping tablespoon matzoh meal

1 medium onion, finely grated

¼ teaspoon baking powder

applesauce

sour cream

- Combine potatoes, eggs, salt, matzoh meal, onion, and baking powder.
- Drop by tablespoonfuls onto a hot greased griddle.
- Fry until both sides are browned.
- Serve with applesauce and sour cream.

Yield: 4 servings

Rendered goose fat used to be a staple kept in every Jewish home in Europe. It was replaced by chicken fat in this country, and that in turn has been replaced by vegetable oils or margarine due to health concerns.

However, studies have shown that people living in the areas of France where geese are raised and eaten show low incidences of heart disease. Also, chemical analysis of goose fat shows similarities to olive oil, which is considered healthful.

Everyone Loves Kugel

Mrs. Zuckerman's Kugel   Robin Angel * Maitland, Florida

12 ounces thin egg noodles

6 eggs, beaten

1 cup sugar

1 pound cream-style cottage cheese

8 ounces farmer cheese

4 ounces cream cheese

1 cup sour cream

2 cups milk

6 tablespoons butter, melted

1 teaspoon vanilla

1 teaspoon salt

cinnamon sugar

- Preheat oven to 350° F. Grease a 9 x 13-inch kugel dish.
- Cook noodles. Add eggs, sugar, cottage cheese, farmer cheese, cream cheese, sour cream, milk, butter, vanilla, and salt.
- Put noodle mixture into kugel dish. Sprinkle generous amount of cinnamon sugar over top.
- Bake for 1 hour, until kugel starts to brown.

Yield: 12 servings

The setting for the play "Beau Jest" by James Herman is a table where a Jewish meal is served. The noodle pudding that was served during the meal on stage was so much a part of the plot of the play and the evening's total theater experience that portions of the kugel (with cinnamon and raisins) were sold in the lobby during intermission—one dollar each—when the play was performed at the Lambs Theater on West 44th Street in New York City.

Apple Cherry Noodle Kugel Debra M. Dalin ✳ Cooper City, Florida

1 21-ounce can apple pie filling

1 21-ounce can cherry or peach pie filling

1 cup sugar

½ pound margarine, melted

4 eggs, beaten

1½ cups raisins

⅛ teaspoon cinnamon

1 pound noodles, cooked and drained

cinnamon, to taste

sugar, to taste

- Preheat oven to 325° F. Grease a 9 x 13-inch baking pan.
- Combine apple pie filling, cherry pie filling, 1 cup sugar, margarine, eggs, raisins, and ⅛ teaspoon cinnamon. Stir well. Add noodles and gently stir again.
- Pour kugel into baking pan.
- Sprinkle cinnamon and sugar over top.
- Bake for 1 hour.
- Kugel can be frozen.

Yield: 12 servings

Challah Kugel Tzippi Rosen ✳ Forest Hills, New York

1 medium to large challah, broken into
  pieces
1 cup boiling water
1 medium onion, chopped
1 green pepper, chopped
1 to 2 tablespoons oil

½ teaspoon garlic powder
1 teaspoon onion powder
dash of paprika
1 to 2 eggs (depending on amount of
  challah)
2 cups clear chicken broth

- Preheat oven to 350° F.
- Pour boiling water over challah pieces. Add additional boiling water if necessary until challah is softened. Set aside.
- Sauté onion and green pepper in oil. Mix with challah. Add garlic powder, onion powder, paprika, egg(s), and chicken broth. Mix together well.
- Put into a 2- or 3-quart baking dish.
- Bake uncovered for 1 to 1½ hours.

Yield: 6 to 8 servings

Round challahs are traditional on Rosh Hashanah to symbolize the cyclical and eternal nature of life, expressing the hope that the coming year will be complete, unbroken by tragedy.

Noodle Pudding   Diane Engel ✳ Branchburg, New Jersey

¾ *pound wide noodles*

3 egg yolks

1 cup sugar

1 cup sour cream

½ *pound cottage cheese or pot cheese*

½ *cup golden raisins*

5 egg whites, beaten until stiff but not
  too dry

cinnamon

- Preheat oven to 350° F.
- Parboil noodles according to package directions. Drain and rinse under cold water. Set aside.
- In a large mixing bowl, combine egg yolks, sugar, and sour cream. Blend. With a large ladle, blend in cottage cheese and raisins, mixing gently. Fold in cooked noodles. Fold in egg whites.
- Pour noodle mixture into an ungreased 9 x 13-inch glass pan.
- Sprinkle cinnamon over top.
- Bake for 40 minutes, until golden brown.
- Remove from oven, let cool completely, and cut into serving size pieces while pudding is still in pan.
- If pudding is being made in advance and not going to be served as soon as it is made, bake for only 30 minutes instead of 40 minutes. When ready to serve, cut pudding into pieces, cover so it will not dry out, and reheat at low temperature until warmed.

Yield: 12 servings

Good-For-You Applesauce Kugel   Karen Fischer Factor ✳ Durham, North Carolina

8 ounces ¼-inch noodles, cooked and
    drained

4 egg whites, or ½ cup Egg Beaters

2 eggs

½ cup oil

2 cups applesauce

¼ cup raisins

¾ cup sugar

¼ teaspoon cinnamon

½ teaspoon salt

cinnamon for sprinkling

sugar for sprinkling

- Preheat oven to 400° F. Grease a 9 x 13-inch baking pan.
- Combine noodles, egg whites, eggs, oil, applesauce, raisins, sugar, cinnamon, and salt. Mix together very well.
- Pour into baking pan.
- Sprinkle with cinnamon and sugar.
- Bake for 45 minutes.

Yield: 12 servings

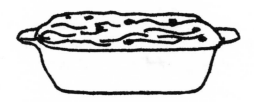

Chubby's Favorite Noodle Kugel

Melissa Ann Simmons * Cincinnati, Ohio

8 ounces broad noodles

½ pound butter

4 ounces cream cheese

1 cup cottage cheese

1 cup sour cream

1 egg

½ cup milk

salt, if desired

pepper, if desired

Ingredients for Fat-Free or Light Version

8 ounces broad noodles

¼ pound light margarine

4 ounces light cream cheese

1 cup fat-free or light cottage cheese

1 cup fat-free or light sour cream

Egg Beaters equivalent to 1 egg

½ cup skim milk

salt, if desired

pepper, if desired

- Preheat oven to 350° F.
- Parboil noodles until almost tender. Drain well and transfer to a large bowl.
- While noodles are hot, add butter (or margarine) and cream cheese. Mix until melted. Add cottage cheese, sour cream, egg, and milk, mixing together well.
- Pour into a casserole dish.
- Bake for 30 to 45 minutes, until bubbly and top starts to brown.
- Serve hot, with salt and pepper, if desired.

Yield: 6 to 8 servings

Best-Ever Cheese Noodle Kugel Brenda Altschul ✳ Framingham, Massachusetts

4 cups regular or yolk-free noodles,
   medium or broad

10 slices thick American cheese, such as
   Kraft Old English or Kraft Deluxe,
   not individually wrapped

2 eggs

2 cups milk, skim to whole

12 ounces cottage cheese, any type

- Preheat oven to 350° F. Grease a 9 x 12 x 2-inch baking pan.
- Cook noodles according to package directions. Rinse under cold water and drain. Set aside.
- On a cutting board, group cheese slices into two stacks of five pieces. With a very sharp knife, cut the cheese first crosswise and then lengthwise into very small pieces. Set aside.
- In a medium bowl, beat eggs with electric beaters for 2 minutes on high until eggs are frothy. Add milk and stir. Set aside.
- Combine noodles, cottage cheese, and American cheese pieces. Add to egg and milk mixture, stirring well.
- Pour into baking pan.
- Bake uncovered for approximately 1½ hours, until top is medium brown.
- Remove from oven and let cool for 5 to 10 minutes.
- Cut into squares, large size for main dish accompaniment or small size for appetizers.

Yield: 12 main dish servings or 24 appetizer servings

Sweet Finales

Applesauce Honey Cake   Wendy Rhomberg * Columbia, Missouri

1 pound honey

3 eggs, beaten

1½ cups sugar

1 cup applesauce

1 cup whole berry cranberry sauce

4 cups flour

1 teaspoon baking soda

1 teaspoon cinnamon

½ teaspoon nutmeg

1 cup chopped candied fruit

- Preheat oven to 350° F. Grease 2 loaf pans and line with waxed paper.
- Mix together honey and eggs. Stir in sugar, applesauce, and cranberry sauce. Sift flour, baking soda, cinnamon, and nutmeg and add to honey mixture. Stir in candied fruits.
- Pour batter into loaf pans.
- Bake for 50 to 60 minutes.

Yield: 16 servings

The custom of eating honey on Rosh Hashanah represents the hope for sweetness in the coming year for all Jews.

Honey cake, a Rosh Hashanah tradition, is called "lekach," a Hebrew word meaning "portion." It is served with the hope and prayer that those who observe Jewish traditions will be blessed with "a goodly portion."

In addition, it is common practice to avoid sour foods during Rosh Hashanah.

Raisin-Chocolate Chip Meringues Leslie Kohn * St. Louis, Missouri

¼ cup small chocolate chips

¼ cup raisins

⅔ cup sugar

2 whites of large eggs

⅛ teaspoon cream of tarter

dash of salt

- Preheat oven to 350° F. Grease a cookie sheet.
- Combine chocolate chips, raisins, and 2 tablespoons of the sugar. Set aside.
- Beat the egg whites until very stiff. Beat in cream of tarter and salt. Gradually add remaining sugar, a little at a time. Fold in chocolate chip mixture.
- Drop by tablespoonfuls onto cookie sheet about 1 inch apart.
- Place in oven and immediately turn off heat. Leave cookies in oven without opening oven door for at least 8 hours or overnight.

Yield: about 2 dozen meringues

Min Weinstein's Mandel Brate

Donna R. Weinstein ✳ Basking Ridge, New Jersey

¾ cup peanut oil

1 cup sugar

3 eggs

juice of ½ lemon or 1 tablespoon lemon
   juice

2 teaspoons potato starch

1½ cups matzoh cake meal

1 cup almonds or walnuts

sugar for sprinkling

- Preheat oven to 350° F. Grease a cookie sheet.
- Mix together peanut oil, sugar, eggs, and lemon juice. Set aside.
- Sift together potato starch and matzoh cake meal. Add to sugar and egg mixture. Fold in almonds or walnuts.
- Divide batter into two or three portions. Form each portion into 2-inch wide strips. The dough can be hard to handle so wet hands before rolling it into strips or put the dough on waxed paper first, coating the dough and/or the waxed paper with a little matzoh cake meal.
- Place strips on cookie sheet.
- Bake for 40 minutes.
- Remove from oven and cut strips into diagonal bars. Turn bars on their sides, sprinkle with sugar, and return to oven for 5 more minutes.
- Let cool before storing.

Yield: 3 to 4 dozen bars

The variety of prepared kosher dishes available in stores is mind-boggling, with choices not even dreamed of ten years ago.

Some of the foods observant Jews can enjoy are:

* Shiitake Mushroom Rice, a mix of mushrooms, soy sauce, and molasses
* Teriyaki Fried Rice with a blend of soy sauce, onion, ginger, lemon, and lime
* Smokey Cowboy Beans with black beans, chilies, sweet peppers, and a touch of cilantro
* Vegetarian Eggplant Rollettes, lightly breaded slices of eggplant stuffed with tofu, spinach, and broccoli and topped with marinara sauce
* Indian dishes with lentils, chick peas, green peas, rice, and a blend of Indian herbs and spices
* Italian, New England, Polynesian, Mexican, and Texan barbecue sauces
* extra chunky salsa, both mild and hot
* artichoke and capers pasta sauce
* apple cinnamon, blueberry almond, chocolate fudge, and peanut butter energy bars.

Sour Cream Coffee Cake Natale Giddings * University City, Missouri

4 tablespoons butter or margarine, softened

1 cup sugar

2 eggs, beaten

2 cups flour

1 teaspoon baking powder

¼ teaspoon salt

1 teaspoon vanilla

1 cup sour cream

Walnut Topping (recipe follows)

- Preheat oven to 350° F. Grease and flour an 8- or 9-inch square pan.
- Cream butter and sugar. Mix in eggs. Set aside.
- Sift together flour, baking powder, and salt. Set aside.
- Mix together vanilla and sour cream.
- Add flour mixture alternately with sour cream mixture to butter mixture.
- Pour half of batter into greased pan. Sprinkle ¾ cup of walnut topping over batter in pan. Spoon remaining half of batter over topping and then sprinkle remaining walnut topping over batter.
- Bake for 50 to 60 minutes, until cake tests clean with a toothpick.
- (If using a glass pan, bake at 325°F.)
- Let cool and then cut into 2-inch squares.

Yield: 16 servings

Walnut Topping

½ cup chopped walnuts
½ cup brown sugar

1 teaspoon cinnamon

- Mix together walnuts, sugar, and cinnamon.

Baron Rothschild was well known for his enormous support and generous philanthropy to Israel, starting with the first Jewish settlers in Palestine in the 1800s. With his backing, grapes were grown and wine was made.

Despite that early involvement in making wine in Palestine, there was a 100-year hiatus in producing fine kosher wine that was finally ended in 1989.

On a cold winter day in that year a pallet was unloaded from a ship onto a pier in New Jersey with 350 cases of the first kosher Rothschild Bordeaux in 100 years and the first ever to come to the United States.

For the wine merchants standing on the pier and shivering in the cold, it was truly a simcha and they broke out in spontaneous applause as the crane gently set the pallet down onto the ground.

Almond-Cherry Macaroons Vicky Lenneman ✳ Lauderdale, Minnesota

2 tablespoons flour

½ cup sugar

½ teaspoon salt

2 egg whites

½ teaspoon almond flavoring

½ cup chopped candied cherries

2 cups flaked coconut

- Preheat oven to 350° F. Grease a cookie sheet.
- Mix together flour, sugar, and salt and sift.
- Beat egg whites until stiff and fold into flour mixture. Stir in almond flavoring, cherries, and coconut.
- Drop by teaspoonfuls onto cookie sheet about 2 inches apart.
- Bake for 15 to 20 minutes, until golden brown.

Yield: about 20 2-inch macaroons

"Two-Cup" Tangy Melon Balls Ronald Deutsch ✳ St. Paul, Minnesota

2 cups cantaloupe balls

2 cups honeydew balls

2 cups watermelon balls

2 cups banana slices

2 cups pineapple chunks

¾ cup Sabra Liqueur (orange liqueur)

■ Place cantaloupe balls, honeydew balls, watermelon balls, banana slices, and pineapple chunks in a large bowl. Pour liqueur over top and stir until fruits and liqueur are evenly distributed.

Yield: 6 to 8 servings

There is a logical reason why a restaurant in the Neveh Iun area of Israel near Jerusalem is called the Elvis Inn.

The King was Jewish. Not just King David and King Solomon, but Elvis Aron Presley also.

In the book *Elvis and Gladys* by Elaine Diundy, the author notes that Elvis's maternal great-great-grandmother Nancy Trackett was Jewish and she had an unbroken string of daughters; Nancy had Martha who had Doll who had Gladys—who, of course, had Elvis.

What better tribute to a famous Jewish singer than having a restaurant named after him. In Israel.

Everyone's Favorite
Jewish Apple Cake Ruth Strauss * Charleston, South Carolina

4 eggs, separated

1 cup sugar

juice of 1 lemon

1 cup flour

6 to 8 apples, peeled, cored, sliced, and put into a bowl of water with a spritz of lemon juice

2 to 3 tablespoons butter or margarine, melted

dash of nutmeg

1½ to 2 teaspoons cinnamon mixed with 3 tablespoons sugar

- Preheat oven to 350° F. Grease a 9-inch springform pan and dust with flour.
- Beat egg yolks with 1 cup sugar until light in color and creamy. Add lemon juice and flour, beating well. Set aside.
- Beat egg whites until stiff and fold into sugar mixture.
- Pour half the batter into the springform pan.
- Drain apple slices and spread half of the slices evenly on top of batter in pan. Brush apple slices with half of the melted butter. Sprinkle nutmeg and half of cinnamon and sugar mixture over top.
- Pour remaining batter on top of apple layer in pan and arrange remaining apple slices on top. Brush remaining butter on apple slices and sprinkle with remaining cinnamon and sugar mixture.
- Bake for about 1 hour.

Yield: 6 to 8 servings

Fruit Tzimmes Donna Winter * East Lansing, Michigan

1½ pounds dried fruits (pears, apricots,
    cranberries, raisins, prunes, figs,
    peaches)

½ cup brown rice

¼ cup honey

½ teaspoon cinnamon

dash of salt

2 cups boiling water

Fruit Juice Sauce (recipe follows)

■   Mix together dried fruits, rice, honey, cinnamon, and salt. Place in a pot and cover with boiling water.

■   Bring again to boiling, then reduce heat and simmer slowly for about 30 minutes, until the rice is tender. If necessary, a little extra water may be added.

■   Pour fruit juice sauce over top and cook over low heat, with gentle stirring, for 5 to 10 minutes, until the liquid has thickened and the tzimmes is thoroughly mixed.

Yield: 6 to 8 servings

Fruit Juice Sauce

2 tablespoons flour

2 tablespoons margarine

1 cup fruit juice (orange, juice, apple
    juice, grape juice, pineapple juice, or
    any combination)

■   Heat flour in a skillet until lightly browned. Stir in margarine and then slowly stir in fruit juice, mixing together gently to prevent lumps. Continue cooking until sauce has thickened.

Chocolate Tofu Pie Roberta Elford ✳ Richmond, Virginia

2 12-ounce packages silken tofu

12 ounces semisweet chocolate, melted

1 teaspoon vanilla

Graham Cracker Pie Crust (recipe follows), or prepared 9-inch graham cracker pie crust

- Blend tofu in food processor until smooth. Add melted chocolate and vanilla. Blend until thoroughly mixed.
- Pour filling into graham cracker crust.
- Chill in refrigerator for at least 4 hours.

Yield: 10 servings

Graham Cracker Pie Crust

8 whole chocolate graham crackers, crushed to equal 1 cup

2 tablespoons brown sugar

4 tablespoons butter or margarine, melted

- Preheat oven to 325° F.
- Combine graham cracker crumbs, sugar, and butter.
- Press crust onto bottom and sides of a 9-inch pie plate.
- Bake for 10 minutes.

Walnut and Raisin Rugelach Ellen Baliff * East Brunswick, New Jersey

½ pound butter, softened

2 cups flour

6 ounces cream cheese, softened

1 tablespoon cinnamon

approximately 1 cup confectioners' sugar

1 cup dark brown sugar

½ cup chopped walnuts

½ cup raisins

egg yolks, optional

- Cream butter and then add flour. Mix well. Add cream cheese and cinnamon and mix again thoroughly.
- Divide dough into 3 balls, wrap each ball in waxed paper, and refrigerate for at least 2 hours.
- Preheat oven to 350° F.
- Cover a surface with confectioners' sugar to prevent dough from sticking. One at a time roll out dough balls into a circle. Turn dough over several times while rolling out to absorb sugar and keep dough from sticking to surface.
- Reapply confectioners' sugar to surface after each ball is completed or as needed to prevent sticking.
- Sprinkle each dough circle with a third of the brown sugar, walnuts, and raisins.
- Divide dough circles into 8 to 10 wedges. Roll up the wedges, starting from the wide side, into crescent shapes.
- Brush with egg yolk, if desired.
- Place rugelach on ungreased cookie sheets.
- Bake for 15 to 18 minutes, or until lightly browned.
- Rugelach can be frozen.

Yield: 24 to 30 pieces

Hamantashen Vicky Sokoloff * Fleetwood, Pennsylvania

1 cup sugar

¼ pound butter

3 eggs

1 teaspoon vanilla

1 cup flour

1½ teaspoons baking powder

¼ teaspoon salt

½ teaspoon grated orange rind

assorted fruit preserves

- Cream sugar and butter together. Add eggs and vanilla. Set aside.
- In a separate bowl, combine flour, baking powder, salt, and orange rind. Add to sugar mixture and knead lightly until smooth.
- Refrigerate for 1 hour.
- Preheat oven to 350° F. Lightly grease 2 cookie sheets.
- Roll out dough to ⅛-inch thickness and cut into 3½-inch rounds.
- Put a heaping teaspoon of your favorite fruit preserve in the center of each dough round.
- Fold up the sides of the dough to form a triangle, pinching the edges well to hold the shape.
- Place hamantashen on cookie sheets.
- Bake for 20 minutes.

Yield: 36 hamantashen

According to some scholars, both hamantashen and kreplach are made with three corners—triangular shape—to represent the three patriarchs, Abraham, Isaac, and Jacob, the founders of the Jewish way of life.

There is no evidence that the three-sided hamantashen is meant to represent the type of hat worn by Haman.

Apricot-Apple Crisp Lisa Towler ✳ Ann Arbor, Michigan

3 cups pitted and sliced apricots

2 cups cored, peeled, and sliced apples

¼ cup sugar

½ cup rolled oats

¾ cup brown sugar

¼ cup flour

½ teaspoon cinnamon

4 tablespoons margarine, softened

½ cup chopped pecans

▪ Preheat oven to 375° F.

▪ Place apricot and apple slices in an 8- or 9-inch pie dish. Sprinkle sugar over top. Set aside.

▪ Mix together oats, brown sugar, flour, and cinnamon. Cut in margarine until crumbly. Mix in pecans. Sprinkle over apricot and apple slices.

▪ Bake for 30 to 35 minutes, until fruit is soft and pecan topping is golden brown.

Yield: 6 servings

Grandma's Strudel   Amy Francer * Hopedale, Massachusetts

2¼ cups flour

1 tablespoon sugar

½ pound butter, melted

1 cup sour cream

12 ounces apricot preserves, or 12 ounces chocolate chips, or ½ to ¾ cup golden raisins and ½ cup walnuts, chopped

cinnamon sugar

- Combine flour, sugar, butter, and sour cream and mix well, using fork and hands.
- Chill in refrigerator until easy to handle.
- Preheat oven to 325° to 350° F. Grease a cookie sheet.
- Roll out dough on a floured surface into a rectangle approximately 9 x 13 inches.
- Spread apricot preserves or chocolate chips or raisins and walnuts on top of dough rectangle.
- Roll up the 13-inch side of the dough and sprinkle with cinnamon sugar.
- Place strudel on cookie sheet.
- Bake for approximately 45 minutes until lightly crisp.
- Remove from oven and cut into slices.
- Add more fillings, if desired.

Yield: approximately 12 slices

Hanukkah Apple Sauce Bessie Frankel ∗ Honolulu, Hawaii

16 apples, any combination of varieties
½ cup dried cranberries
1 cup water
¾ cup sugar

¼ cup brown sugar
½ to 1 teaspoon cinnamon
dash of nutmeg

- Cut apples into quarters and remove core. Place in a large heavy pot along with cranberries and water. Cover.
- Heat to boiling. Reduce heat to a simmer and cook for about 15 minutes more, until apples and cranberries are soft.
- Remove from heat and remove apples from pot. Set aside cranberries and water remaining in pot.
- Press apples through a fine strainer often. Discard apple skins that remain in strainer.
- Mix strained apples with cranberries and water remaining in pot. Add sugar, brown sugar, cinnamon, and nutmeg, mixing thoroughly.
- Serve warm or chill in refrigerator and serve cold.

Yield: 6 to 8 servings

New Year's Honey Cake   Selma Lachman * Tacoma, Washington

4 eggs

2 cups sugar

½ cup oil

½ cup shortening

*2 teaspoons baking soda dissolved in 1
    cup strong coffee*

2 cups honey

7 cups sifted flour

1½ teaspoons baking powder

½ teaspoon salt

1 teaspoon ground ginger

1 teaspoon ground cloves

1 teaspoon cinnamon

1 8-ounce can crushed pineapple

■   Preheat oven to 325° F. Grease 3 loaf pans and line with waxed paper.

■   Cream eggs and sugar. Add oil, shortening, coffee with dissolved baking soda, and
honey. Mix together well. Set aside.

■   Sift flour, baking powder, salt, ginger, cloves, and cinnamon. Add to honey mixture. Mix in crushed pineapple.

■   Divide batter equally among the loaf pans.

■   Bake for 1 hour and 15 minutes, until a cake tester comes out nearly clean.

Yield: 24 servings

Pure Creamy Cheesecake   Nancy Kashman ✳ New Orleans, Louisiana

6 to 8 graham crackers, crushed

1 pound cream cheese

1 pound ricotta cheese, strained

1 cup sugar

4 eggs

1½ teaspoons lemon juice

1 teaspoon vanilla

1½ teaspoons cornstarch

3 tablespoons flour

¼ pound butter, melted

1 pint sour cream

▪ Press crushed graham crackers onto the bottom of a greased 9-inch springform pan. Set aside in refrigerator.

▪ Preheat oven to 350° F.

▪ Mix together cream cheese and ricotta. Add sugar and eggs, beating well. Add lemon juice, vanilla, cornstarch, and flour. Beat until smooth. Add butter and sour cream. Beat well.

▪ Pour mixture into springform pan.

▪ Bake for about 1 hour, until done.

▪ Turn off heat and leave cheesecake in oven with the door open for about 2 hours.

Yield: 8 to 10 servings

Fruity Mandel Bread Charlotte D. Lastnik * Framingham, Massachusetts

3 large eggs

1 cup sugar

1 cup oil

1 teaspoon vanilla or almond extract

3 cups all-purpose flour, sifted

1 teaspoon baking powder

¼ cup chopped nuts

½ cup chopped dried fruit

- Preheat oven to 350° F. Grease a baking sheet.
- Beat eggs, sugar, oil, and vanilla until well blended. Gradually add flour and baking powder. Add nuts and fruit, mixing well. Batter will be stiff.
- Divide batter into 2 portions and form into long strips. Place both strips on baking sheet, smoothing tops and sides. If necessary, use 2 baking sheets.
- Bake for about 18 minutes.
- Remove from oven, cut strips into diagonal slices, and turn on sides.
- Return to oven and bake for about 15 minutes more, until lightly brown and dry.

Yield: about 40 pieces

Old-Fashioned Pound Cake Toby Katz ✳ Grand Blanc, Michigan

6 eggs

1 pound butter, at room temperature

7½ cups confectioners' sugar, sifted

3 cups cake flour

3 teaspoons vanilla

fresh fruit slices

- Preheat oven to 350° F. Grease a tube pan.
- Beat together eggs, butter, and confectioners' sugar. Add flour and vanilla, mixing thoroughly.
- Put batter in tube pan.
- Bake for 1½ hours.
- Serve with fresh fruit slices.

Yield: 6 to 8 servings

Babooshka's Gefilte Fish Revekka Lazebnik * Philadelphia, Pennsylvania

1 6- to 10-pound carp

1 large onion

2 egg yolks

2 tablespoons Cream of Wheat (enriched farina)

1 tablespoon water

2 tablespoons sugar

salt, to taste

pepper, to taste

1 egg white, beaten

8 to 10 large beets

8 to 10 large carrots

3 small onions

6 to 10 potatoes

fresh dill, optional

- Scale the carp and remove the eyes. (This step could be done at the fish store.)
- Using a very sharp knife, cut the fish vertically into 2-inch to 3-inch chunks. Cut the head the same way, leaving an inch or two below.
- Remove the guts of the carp and clean under cold water.
- Take a sharp, small knife and without piercing the skin slowly cut out the meat, leaving the shell of the chunks intact.
- Place the fish meat in another bowl. Repeat for all the chunks of the fish. (Remember that later you will be restuffing the shells of these chunks with a fish mixture.) When you get to the tail, slide the tail bone out and then cut out the meat.
- In a grinder or a blender, grind the large onion, egg yolk, Cream of Wheat, 1 tablespoon water, 1 tablespoon sugar, and lots of salt and pepper. If you like it spicy, add lots of pepper. Mix in beaten egg white. Set aside.
- Cut beets into circular, semi-thin slices. Next, cut the carrots into ½-inch diagonal chunks. Cut the 3 small onions into circular pieces.

- In a large pan such as used for a stew, layer the bottom with a layer of beets, a layer of carrots, and a layer of onions. Set aside.
- Take the fish shells—the skin should not be pierced if possible—and stuff the fish mixture into them, filling every crevice possible.
- Gently lay two pieces of fish on top of the carrots, beets, and onions.
- Sandwich with another layer of beets, carrots, and onions. Keep repeating until the top of the pan is reached. Add salt, pepper, and the remaining 1 tablespoon sugar. Add water almost to the top.
- Boil on high heat for 20 minutes, on medium heat for 1 hour, and on low heat for 1 more hour.
- Let cool for 3 hours.
- Gently remove each piece of fish from the pan and place on a platter, reconstructing the original shape of the fish, including the head and tail.
- Arrange pieces of beets and carrots, enveloping the fish. Do not discard the liquid, leaving some onions, beets, and carrots in the mixture. Cover and refrigerate.
- Cut potatoes into wedges and boil until cooked. You should be able to slide a fork inside without the potatoes falling apart. They should be a bright pink. Take out and lay on the same platter as the fish.
- Pour some of the liquid on top of the fish masterpiece. Do not totally cover the fish, maybe an inch or two, since this is the stuff that jells. Refrigerate overnight.
- If there is not enough room on the fish platter for the potatoes, put them in a separate bowl. Cover with some of the liquid along with some beets and carrots.
- Discard the rest of the liquid.
- Serve cold.
- If desired, sprinkle fresh dill over top prior to serving.

Yield: 4 to 6 servings

Horseradish Dip Sid Cohen ✳ Cincinnati, Ohio

½ cup prepared horseradish
1 cup pineapple preserves
1 cup apple jelly
2 tablespoons dry mustard

lemon slices, parsley, or mint for garnish
crackers, optional
cream cheese, optional

- Drain horseradish. Combine with pineapple preserves, apple jelly, and dry mustard.
- Chill in refrigerator.
- Garnish with lemon slices, parsley, or mint.
- If desired, serve on crackers with cream cheese.

Yield: 3 cups

Right along with Amazon.com, Priceline.com, and eBay.com, there is a place in cyberspace for the kosher shopper who wants to get kosher foods but is too far away from a store selling acceptable products.

Just click onto The Kosher Supermarket at http://www.koshersupermarket.com and a world of kosher foods is there waiting to be delivered to your door for you to enjoy.

Mock Chopped Liver Mae Goldman ✳ Charlotte, North Carolina

1 16-ounce can LeSeur tiny peas

3 medium onions

canola oil

4 hard-boiled eggs

¾ cup chopped walnuts

salt, to taste

pepper, to taste

- ▪ Drain peas and set aside.
- ▪ Sauté onions in canola oil.
- ▪ Combine drained peas, sautéed onions, 1 whole hard-boiled egg and the whites of the other 3 hard-boiled eggs, walnuts, salt, and pepper. Mix in a food processor until desired consistency is reached.
- ▪ This dish can be frozen.

Yield: 4 to 6 servings

Kosher Pickles or Tomatoes Norm Marcovitch ∗ Garden Grove, California

6 quarts water

2 cups kosher salt (recommended) or 1 cup pickling salt

24 to 30 medium-size pickling cucumbers or 24 to 30 firm green tomatoes

3 1½ to 2-ounce packages pickling spices

36 large garlic cloves

6 large sprigs of fresh dill

¾ cup white vinegar

12 to 18 hot red peppers

- Bring water to boiling and add salt. Cook until salt has dissolved.
- Remove from heat and allow to cool.
- Place 4 to 6 pickles or tomatoes in each of 6 1-quart jars. In each jar place ½ package pickling spices, 6 garlic cloves, 1 dill sprig, and 2 tablespoons white vinegar. For spicier pickles or tomatoes, add 2 or 3 red peppers to each jar.
- Fill the 6 jars with the cooled brine (salt water).
- Seal and store the jars in a dark place for 8 days for pickles or 2 to 3 weeks for tomatoes. Cure according to taste.
- Refrigerate jars after curing.

Yield: 24 to 30 pickles or pickled tomatoes

Mom's "Secret" Chopped Liver Howard H. Levinson ✳ Durham, North Carolina

1 pound calf's or beef liver, finely
   chopped

3 to 4 hard-boiled eggs, finely chopped

1 sweet onion, diced

1 celery stalk, diced

1 soft-boiled egg yolk

iceberg lettuce leaves

salt, to taste

pepper, to taste

■ Combine liver, hard-boiled eggs, onion, celery, and egg yolk, mixing together well. Use less or more than a whole egg yolk depending on the consistency of the chopped liver that is desired.

■ Serve on iceberg lettuce leaves.

■ Put salt and pepper to taste on individual servings.

Yield: 4 servings

There is a connection between French gourmet cuisine and traditional Jewish food.
   Paté de foie gras, the famous French dish made from the livers of fattened geese, has its origins in the chopped liver made by European Jews.

Barsky's Blintzes
Naomi Barsky ✳ New York, New York

Pancakes

⅔ cup water

1¼ cups milk (regular or skim)

1 cup flour

2 eggs

salt, to taste

1 tablespoon oil

oil for frying

Filling

1 pound cottage cheese (regular or low fat)

½ pound cream cheese (regular or low fat)

½ cup sugar

1 teaspoon vanilla

Assembly

3 tablespoons unsalted margarine, melted

sour cream

fresh fruit slices

■ Add water and milk to flour, beating well. Add eggs, salt, and 1 tablespoon oil and beat until smooth. Set aside.

■ Heat a 6- to 8-inch nonstick frying pan that has been greased with oil.

■ Pour about ¼ cup of batter, enough to cover the bottom, into pan. Fry until batter forms a thin sheet, then turn over onto waxed paper.

■ For the filling, mix together cottage cheese, cream cheese, sugar, and vanilla.

■ Preheat oven to 350° to 375° F. Grease a cookie sheet.

■ Spread 1 to 2 tablespoons of filling on each pancake. Fold edges of pancake over filling, turn sides in, and roll up into a long roll.

■ Brush blintzes with margarine and place on cookie sheet.

■ Bake for about 20 minutes, until blintzes are golden.

■ Serve with sour cream and fresh fruit slices.

Yield: 12 servings

Momma Ronna's No-Fuss
Chopped Chicken Livers Ronna Schneir * Santa Monica, California

2 cups (about 1 pound) chicken livers

⅓ cup finely chopped onion

2 large hard-boiled eggs, chopped

¼ cup finely chopped celery

1 tablespoon minced fresh garlic

1 teaspoon (more or less to taste) Lawrys
Seasoned Salt

1 tablespoon Worcestershire Sauce

1 tablespoon ranch-style salad dressing
(can be eliminated to keep recipe
kosher)

celery, if desired

crackers, if desired

- Place chicken livers in a medium-size microwave-safe bowl or dish. Microwave on High for 4 minutes. Turn once and drain juices after 2 minutes. Cook chicken livers until they are light pink inside. Cool in refrigerator.
- When chicken livers are cool enough to handle, cut membranes with a knife and fork.
- Add in onion, hard-boiled eggs, celery, garlic, Lawrys Seasoned Salt, Worcestershire Sauce, and ranch-style salad dressing. Using your hands or a fork, mix together until thoroughly blended.
- Chill in refrigerator.
- Serve by itself or with celery or crackers.

Yield: 4 servings

Mock Gefilte Fish Balls Pamela Lasserson ✳ Syracuse, New York

1 14.75-ounce can pink salmon, drained

2 large eggs, beaten

½ teaspoon salt

¼ teaspoon garlic powder

¼ teaspoon pepper

1 onion, peeled and grated

¼ cup matzoh meal

2 onions, peeled and sliced

3 carrots, sliced

2 cups water

- Place salmon in a large bowl. Add eggs, salt, garlic powder, and pepper. Mix in grated onion and matzoh meal. Set aside.
- In a saucepan, place the sliced onions, carrots, and water. Heat to boiling, then lower heat to a simmer.
- Form salmon mixture into 1-inch balls. Gently place fish balls in the heated water. Increase heat once more to a boil, then lower heat to medium. Cover and cook for 20 to 30 minutes.
- Remove from heat and let cool for 15 minutes. Place fish balls in a bowl and chill in refrigerator before serving.
- Garnish fish balls with cooked carrots, cut into circles.

Yield: 4 servings

Gefilte fish became a traditional dish for the Sabbath for two reasons. First, it was considered a glamorous dish because the fish was stuffed. Second, some versions of gefilte fish had the bones already removed so you did not have to remove them on the Sabbath, an activity that could be considered to be work and, therefore, forbidden on that day.

Liver Knishes Mollie Schindle ✳ Fresh Meadows, New York

2 cups mashed potatoes	2 eggs
¼ cup matzoh meal	prepared chopped liver
½ teaspoon salt	beaten eggs
dash of pepper	oil for frying

- Mix together potatoes, matzoh meal, salt, pepper, and eggs. Form into balls.
- Make a hole in the center of the balls and fill with chopped liver.
- Re-form top of potato balls to enclose chopped liver.
- Dip balls in beaten egg.
- Fry in oil until brown.

Yield: 6 to 8 knishes

Knishes, so enjoyed as a delicacy or as an hors d'oeuvre at bar mitzvahs and weddings, have a rather unglamorous origin.

They were originally made and eaten in Europe to give variety to the daily diet of potatoes eaten by poor Jews.

Even in America during the early 1900s, the knish was viewed as a staple, an easy-to-eat, easy-to-carry food that was brought by sweatshop workers every day for lunch.

Chopped Herring Lucy Morris ∗ Portland, Maine

2 whole herrings

2 slices challah bread or other egg or
white bread

½ cup apple cider vinegar

1 large mild onion, peeled and cut into
quarters

2 hard-boiled eggs

dash of pepper

1 to 2 teaspoons mayonnaise

crackers

- Wash herrings under cold water. Remove head, fins, and tail. Split belly and remove entrails. It is not necessary to remove the bones. Rinse inside well. Soak in cold water for 3 to 4 hours, making sure herrings are completely covered with water.
- Soak bread in vinegar. Set aside.
- Place herring, onion, hard-boiled eggs, and apple in a food processor and finely grind. Remove bread from vinegar, squeeze dry, and add to herring mixture. Mix in thoroughly. Add pepper and mayonnaise, mixing together well.
- Serve with crackers.

Yield: 4 servings

Easy "Homemade" Gefilte Fish   Martin Schwartz ✳ Sante Fe, New Mexico

2 large red onions, unpeeled but with
    ends cut off

2 large tomatoes, cubed

2 tablespoons sugar

2 celery stalks

2 large carrots, sliced

dash of salt

dash of pepper

1 2-pound jar prepared gefilte fish pieces

carrots

horseradish

- In a large pot, place onions, tomatoes, sugar, celery stalks, carrots, salt, and pepper. Heat to boiling.
- Add gefilte fish pieces and simmer for about 1½ hours.
- Remove from heat.
- Remove celery and onion skins.
- Chill in refrigerator.
- Serve with carrot slices and horseradish.

Yield: 6 to 8 servings

The origin of gefilte fish is partly financial. It was expected that all Jewish homes serve fish at least once during the Sabbath, but fish was very expensive.

By mixing the fish with other ingredients, it could be extended to serve more than if it were just fish alone.

East Side New York
Half-Sour Pickles Frank Kachman ✳ Valley Stream, New York

30 to 35 small Kirby cucumbers

2 quarts water

½ cup salt

3 ounces mixed pickling spices

3 garlic cloves, smashed

- Fill a 1-gallon jar with cucumbers. Set aside.
- In a separate container, mix together water, salt, pickling spices, and garlic. Pour over cucumbers and then cover with waxed paper to keep cucumbers in solution.
- Leave out for 2 weeks without refrigeration.

Yield: 30 to 35 pickles

Ed Levine, a food writer and author of *New York Eats (More)*, once explained how you can tell if a deli is real or fake.

A real deli, he says, has a bowl of both sour and half-sour pickles on the table when you sit down. If it's necessary to request pickles, or they do not come until your sandwich does, you are not eating in a real deli.

Another definition of a real deli, according to Levine, is a place that serves pastrami, corned beef brisket, and turkey sandwiches too thick to eat, a minimum of six inches high.

Homemade Lox Snooky Lachman Simon ✳ Tacoma, Washington

3 tablespoons uniodized salt

2 tablespoons brown or white sugar

1 teaspoon liquid smoke

2 tablespoons canola oil

2½ pounds fresh wild salmon fillet, skin on, tail section to middle of fish preferred

1 teaspoon fresh dill

- Make a paste of salt, brown sugar, liquid smoke, and canola oil.
- Rub paste into both sides of fish. Sprinkle fresh dill on side of fish without skin.
- Place fish in a self-sealing plastic bag and place bag in a glass pan. Refrigerate for 10 days to 2 weeks. Turn bag over every day.
- Remove from refrigerator, unwrap, and remove excess paste.
- Slice and enjoy with cream cheese, bagels, and onion.
- Lox can be frozen.

Yield: 6 to 8 servings

The bagel name comes from the German word for bracelet while the round shape–with no beginning and no end–symbolizes the eternal cycle of life.

Our Favorite Knishes Aileen Adams * Lincoln, Nebraska

2½ cups flour
¼ cup sugar
⅛ teaspoon salt
¼ cup plus 2 tablespoons vegetable oil
2 eggs, beaten
½ cup warm water

flour for dusting bowl and sprinkling on
    kneading surface
margarine, melted
Liver Filling (recipe follows)
Potato Filling (recipe follows)
vegetable oil or melted margarine

▪ Sift together flour, sugar, and salt. Push down and make a well in the center of the flour mixture and add vegetable oil, eggs, and water, mixing together well.

▪ Dust a bowl with flour and place dough in bowl. Cover with a towel and let stand for about 20 minutes.

▪ Preheat oven to 350°F. Grease 2 cookie sheets until well coated.

▪ Lightly flour a surface and knead dough.

▪ Divide dough in half.

▪ Return one half to the bowl and cover with towel.

▪ Roll out and stretch the other half of the dough into a circle as thin as possible without tearing, about 20 inches in diameter.

▪ Brush with melted margarine.

▪ Put a ring—about 1 inch high and 1½ inches wide—of liver filling or potato filling about 1½ inches in from the outer edges of the dough circle.

▪ Carefully roll up the outer edge of the dough, covering the filling with two layers of dough.

▪ Cut through the dough circle just inside the ring of filled dough, separating the ring from the unused dough.

- Cut ring into 1½- to 2-inch pieces and pinch dough to seal cut ends.
- Continue rolling up dough and filling until all the dough is used up. Brush the tops of the knishes with oil or melted butter.
- Repeat filling process with other half of dough.
- Place knishes on cookie sheets cut sides up and down and, using the palm of your hand, press down so each one is flattened down and round in shape.
- Bake for about 1 hour, until lightly browned.
- Remove from oven and serve hot.

Yield: approximately 30 knishes

Liver Filling

1 medium onion, finely chopped	*1 egg*
1 tablespoon vegetable oil or chicken fat	*¾ teaspoon parsley flakes*
2 cups ground up beef or chicken liver	*salt, to taste*
1 cup mashed potatoes	*pepper, to taste*

- Sauté onion in vegetable oil until golden.
- Thoroughly mix together sautéed onion, ground up liver, mashed potatoes, egg, parsley, salt, and pepper.

Potato Filling

2 medium onions, finely chopped

¼ pound margarine or butter, or ½ cup chicken fat

2 cups mashed potatoes

1 egg

1 teaspoon finely chopped chives

salt, to taste

pepper, to taste

- Sauté onions in margarine until golden.
- Thoroughly mix together sautéed onions, mashed potatoes, egg, chives, salt, and pepper.

It was British mountain climber George Mallory, who died in 1924 on Mount Everest, who said he wanted to climb the world's highest peak "Because it was there."

Now, according to Florence Fabricant, the renowned food writer for *The New York Times*, the knishes sold at Pita Express, a chain of kosher cafés, are the "Mount Everest of Knishes." Weighing in at a hefty three-quarters of a pound and selling for two dollars each, they come filled with potato or spinach.

While other knish shops might offer more variety—broccoli, sweet potatoes, and carrots—and have flakier pastry, Ms. Fabricant says that none of those have the size and good taste of the Pita Express knish.

And, as Ms. Fabricant writes, "You conquer it, not because it was there, but because it was so good."

Chopped Liver with Schmaltz Marshall Kahn ✳ Louisville, Kentucky

6 to 8 large yellow onions, sliced

½ to ¾ cup homemade schmaltz (chicken fat)

salt, to taste

freshly ground pepper, to taste

2 pounds beef or calf's liver, cut into pieces

3 hard-boiled eggs

½ cup chopped fresh parsley

1 medium white radish or daikon

schmaltz for serving (if desired)

▪ In a large heated skillet, sauté 1 to 2 handfuls of onions, enough for 1 layer, in schmaltz, until onions are lightly golden. Sprinkle salt and pepper over liver and place layer of liver in skillet with the onions. Add more schmaltz if needed.

▪ When liver is cooked and onions have caramelized (become soft and golden brown), remove from skillet and let cool.

▪ Repeat process with onion slices and liver until all liver has been cooked. Set aside.

▪ Sauté remaining onions in schmaltz until caramelized. Set aside for garnish.

▪ Grind together cooked liver and onions, eggs, and parsley. Add juices from dish the liver and onions sat on to cool.

▪ Place chopped liver in a ring mold and refrigerate overnight.

▪ To serve, unmold onto a serving dish and surround with extra onions reserved for garnish. Grate radish immediately before serving and place in center of chopped liver mold.

▪ If desired, serve with extra schmaltz on the side.

Yield: 6 to 8 servings

Beyond Matzoh–Passover Delights

Fruit and Nut Charoses Irene Leonard ✳ Seattle, Washington

5 large tart apples, cored, peeled, and
   finely chopped

1 pear, cored, peeled, and finely chopped

1 cup chopped dates

¼ cup chopped prunes

1 cup finely chopped almonds

¼ cup white raisins

½ to ¾ cup honey

1 teaspoon cinnamon

½ teaspoon ginger

1½ to 2 cups Concord grape Passover
   wine

▪ Combine apples, pear, dates, prunes, almonds, raisins, honey, cinnamon, ginger, and wine, mixing together thoroughly.

Yield: about 5 cups

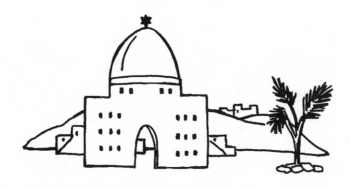

Charoses   Jill Seitz * Eugene, Oregon

6 apples, cored, peeled, and finely
   chopped
1 cup finely chopped walnuts
½ cup finely chopped pecans

1 teaspoon cinnamon
½ cup honey
¼ to ½ cup Passover wine

■   Combine apples, walnuts, pecans, cinnamon, honey, and wine, mixing together thoroughly.

Yield: about 4 cups

Do you like olives? Get ready for olive salt, a condiment that contains powdered olives and garlic. It was developed by the Olivia Food Company of Israel and is meant to be sprinkled on foods like pasta and chicken, giving an instant and intense rush of olive scent and flavor.

    The Olivia Food Company is also marketing olive-branch briquettes for barbecuing, the Mediterranean version of mesquite.

    Contributing to the new foods from Israel that will be found more and more in the United States, Zeta Natural Oils is producing sun-dried souri and barnea olives, both packed in oil just as sun-dried tomatoes are.

Matzoh Brei Jessica Adler ✳ Houston, Texas

1 cup milk

6 matzohs, broken into bite-size pieces

8 eggs, beaten

1 teaspoon onion salt

½ teaspoon garlic salt

margarine for frying

syrup

- Heat milk to very warm but not boiling.
- Remove from heat and put matzoh pieces in milk. Let sit for about 5 minutes.
- Drain and discard milk. Mix together matzoh, eggs, onion salt, and garlic salt.
- Melt margarine in a large frying pan and pour in matzoh mixture.
- Cook over medium heat, stirring occasionally, to desired doneness.
- Serve with syrup.

Yield: 6 servings

Banana-Strawberry
Matzoh Meal Pancakes Bess Diamond ✳ Bellevue, Washington

3 medium to large bananas, mashed

1½ cups cut-up small pieces of strawber-
ries or other fruit as desired

1 cup matzoh meal

1 cup water

light vegetable oil for cooking

syrup

■ Combine mashed bananas, strawberry pieces, matzoh meal, and water, mixing together well.

■ Heat oil on a hot grill. Pour batter onto grill, making 3-inch pancakes.

■ Cook on each side to desired doneness.

■ Serve with syrup.

Yield: 4 servings

Did you ever wonder why matzoh has perforations?

Those tiny holes are made just before the rolled out dough is placed in the oven, in order to allow air to escape during baking, thus slowing down fermentation. The perforations also prevent the
dough from rising and swelling while baking.

And why is matzoh square when it used to be round? This is because a matzoh-making machine
was invented in England in 1875 that made square matzohs, and some of those machines were brought
to the United States.

Passover Matzoh Kugel Gilda Dorfman * Milwaukee, Wisconsin

3 matzohs

water for soaking matzoh

6 egg whites

½ cup sugar

dash of salt

½ teaspoon cinnamon

¼ cup raisins

½ cup chopped almonds

4 apples (tart is best), shredded

grated rind of 1 orange

Cinnamon Sugar (recipe follows)

¼ cup vegetable oil

- Preheat oven to 350°F. Grease a 1½-quart casserole dish.
- Crumble matzohs into water and soak until matzoh is soft. Remove matzoh from water and squeeze dry. Discard water.
- Beat egg whites. Add sugar, salt, and cinnamon, mixing well. Stir in matzoh, raisins, almonds, apples, and orange rind, mixing thoroughly.
- Pour batter into casserole dish. Sprinkle with cinnamon sugar. Pour vegetable oil over top.
- Bake for 40 to 50 minutes, until kugel is firm and lightly browned.

Yield: 6 to 8 servings

Cinnamon Sugar

½ teaspoon cinnamon

1 tablespoon sugar

- Thoroughly mix together cinnamon and sugar.

Passover Apple Cake Mandy Klein * Arlington, Texas

6 eggs

1½ cups sugar

1½ cups matzoh cake meal

⅔ cup vegetable oil

10 to 12 apples, cored, peeled, and sliced
    and coated with ½ cup brown sugar

Walnut Topping (recipe follows)

- Preheat oven to 350°F. Grease a 9 x 13-inch pan.
- Mix together eggs, sugar, and matzoh cake meal. Add in oil, mixing well.
- Pour half of the batter into greased pan.
- Place half of the apple slices on top of the batter in the pan. Pour remaining batter over apple slices in pan and then spread remaining half of the apple slices over top.
- Sprinkle walnut topping over apple slices.
- Bake for 1¼ to 1½ hours. Test cake with a toothpick at 1¼ hours.
- Remove from oven, let cool, and cut into 2-inch squares.

Yield: 2 dozen squares

Walnut Topping

⅓ cup chopped walnuts

½ cup sugar

2 teaspoons cinnamon

- Mix together walnuts, sugar, and cinnamon.

Passover Chocolate Wine Cake
Aileen Mikowstein * Cleveland, Ohio

8 eggs, separated	1 tablespoon potato starch
1½ cups sugar	grated rind of 1 orange
¾ cup matzoh cake meal	juice of 1 orange
3 tablespoons unsweetened cocoa powder	¼ cup heavy sweet Passover wine

- Preheat oven to 325°F. Grease a 9-inch tube pan.
- Beat egg yolks with sugar until creamy and light yellow in color. Set aside.
- Sift together matzoh cake meal, cocoa powder, and potato starch. Stir into egg yolk mixture. Add grated orange rind, orange juice, and wine, stirring well. Set aside.
- Beat egg whites until stiff and then fold into egg yolk mixture.
- Pour batter into tube pan.
- Bake for 50 to 60 minutes. Check at 45 minutes.
- Remove from oven and let sit for 10 minutes. Remove from pan and let cool completely.

Yield: 8 to 10 servings

Chocolate Seder Cake Aaron Siegelman * Brooklyn, New York

8 ounces semisweet chocolate

1 ounce bitter chocolate

2 tablespoons strong decaffeinated coffee

8 eggs, separated

1 cup sugar

dash of salt

cherry liqueur (optional)

- Preheat oven to 350°F. Grease a 9-inch springform pan and sprinkle with sugar.
- Combine semisweet chocolate, bitter chocolate, and coffee and heat over low heat until chocolate has melted. Set aside.
- Beat together egg yolks and sugar until thick and fluffy. Stir into chocolate. Set aside.
- Beat together egg whites and salt until stiff. Fold into chocolate mixture.
- Pour batter into springform pan.
- Bake for 25 to 30 minutes.
- Remove from oven and let stand several minutes before removing cake from pan.
- If desired, pour cherry liqueur over top of hot cake.

Yield: 8 servings

Great Aunt Mildred's Swedish Potato Flour Cookies Made Kosher for Passover Pat Lukens * Sudbury, Massachusetts

½ pound margarine (do not use butter
  since cookies will fall apart)

½ cup sugar

1 cup matzoh cake meal

1 cup potato starch

1 teaspoon vanilla or almond extract

colored sugar, chocolate chips, or
  chopped nuts for decoration

- Preheat oven to 375°F.
- Cream margarine and sugar. Mix in matzoh meal and potato starch. Add vanilla.
- Roll batter into small balls.
- Place on ungreased cookie sheets about 2 inches apart.
- Using a fork, press cookie balls flat. Rotate fork a quarter turn and press again. It is best to dunk fork in water between cookies.
- Decorate tops of cookies with colored sugar, chocolate chips, or chopped nuts.
- Bake for 15 minutes.

Yield: approximately 24 cookies

For those of us of a certain age, the Passover Seder meant a choice of four cups of either Manischewitz Concord grape wine or Mogen David Concord grape wine and that was it.

How times have changed!

While, of course, traditionalists can still drink the old standards, there is a great variety of choices for everyone wanting to have something new and different.

Kedem offers close to twenty Passover wines, including Cream Malaga, Blush Concord, and Matuk Rouge Soft. The Barkan Winery in Israel has Cabernet Sauvignon, Chardonnay, and Merlot.

The Golan Heights Winery, also in Israel, makes Yarden, Golan, and Gamla wines. The Bartenura Winery can grace your Seder table with Moscato d'Asti, Chianti, and Pinot Grigio.

Baron Herzog has an assortment of California wines including Chenin Blanc and white Zinfandel.

And there is even Passover wine made in Hungary. Rashi offers a Tokaji-Furmint from the Tokaji region, one of the most notable wine-growing areas in that European nation. The unique Furmint grapes of that region have attracted the attention of wine lovers around the world.

Passover White Chocolate Cheesecake
Lynne Picard-Landa ✳ South Natick, Massachusetts

Crust

1 cup matzoh meal

3 tablespoons sugar

3 tablespoons margarine

Kahlùa liqueur

Cheese Filling

2 pounds cream cheese

4 eggs

1¼ cups sugar

¾ cup finely chopped white chocolate

¼ cup Kahlùa liqueur

▪ Preheat oven to 350°F.

▪ For the crust, combine matzoh meal, sugar, and margarine. Press onto the bottom of a 10-inch springform pan.

▪ Bake for 10 minutes.

▪ Remove from oven and let cool for several minutes.

▪ When pan is cool, lightly grease the edges above the crust.

▪ If desired, drizzle a small amount of Kahlùa liqueur over the crust for a little extra flavor.

▪ For the filling, combine cream cheese, eggs, and sugar. Mix well. Add white chocolate and liqueur and continue mixing until well blended.

▪ Preheat oven to 350°F.

▪ Place cheese filling on crust in springform pan.

▪ Wrap the outside of the pan with aluminum foil.

▪ Place pan in a baking dish filled with a little water.

- Bake for about 1 hour. Check after 30 minutes to make sure water has not evaporated from the baking dish. Add more water if necessary and continue baking for the remainder of the time.
- Cheesecake is done when it begins to pull away from the edges of the pan.
- Allow cheesecake to cool completely before removing it from the pan.

Yield: 8 servings

Passover is celebrated in three and a half million Jewish households in the United States, making it the most widely celebrated Jewish holiday in this country. Over nine out of ten—92 percent—of all American Jews participate in at least one Seder.

The number of food items labeled "Kosher for Passover" is over sixteen thousand, a greater number than all the kosher products that were available twenty years ago.

Passover Farfel Candy Barbara Schulman ✻ Dallas, Texas

1 pound honey
¼ cup sugar
dash of cinnamon

¾ cup matzoh farfel
2 cups chopped almonds
1 cup chopped walnuts

▪ Place honey and sugar in a heavy saucepan and heat over low heat to boiling. Continue cooking for about 20 minutes more, until mixture turns brown. Remove from heat and stir in cinnamon, matzoh farfel, almonds, and walnuts.

▪ Pour mixture onto a wet cutting board.

▪ Keeping hands wet with very cold water, pat candy into a square ½ to ¾ inch thick.

▪ Let cool and then cut diagonally using a wet knife.

Yield: about 4 dozen candies

Favorites from the Best of Friends and Closest Relatives

California Mediterranean Salad Alison Lentini * East Windsor, New Jersey

1 red pepper, seeded and diced

½ cup kalamata olives, pitted

8 ounces feta cheese, crumbled

10 ounces fresh spinach leaves, torn into
   pieces

3 scallions, chopped

1 pint grape or cherry tomatoes

1 15½-ounce can unseasoned black
   beans, drained and rinsed

Salad Dressing (recipe follows)

- Toss together red pepper, olives, feta cheese, spinach, scallions, tomatoes, and beans.
- Serve with salad dressing.

Yield: 8 servings

Salad Dressing

¼ cup balsamic vinegar

½ cup olive oil

- Mix together vinegar and olive oil.

Eggplant Salad Roni Zisman * Brookline, Massachusetts

1 medium eggplant, skin on, cut into
    quarters
1 green pepper
1 to 2 hard-boiled eggs
1 small onion
salt, to taste

pepper, to taste
1 tablespoon mayonnaise
1 tablespoon olive oil
juice of ½ lemon
4 toasted pita breads

- Cook eggplant in microwave oven for about 10 minutes on high power until soft. Set aside until cool.
- Cook green pepper in microwave oven for about 3 minutes on high power. Set aside until cool.
- Place hard-boiled egg and onion in food processor and pulse until partially chopped. Add cooled eggplant and cooled pepper to processor and pulse until completely chopped.
- Season with salt and pepper. Stir in mayonnaise and olive oil. Add lemon juice and mix thoroughly.
- Chill in refrigerator.
- Serve with toasted pita bread.

Yield: 4 servings

Carrot-Ginger Couscous
Jackie, Craig, and Corina Zisman ∗ Rosendale, New York

1 tablespoon vegetable oil

1 1-inch piece of fresh ginger, peeled and
   grated

¾ cup raisins

4 large carrots, grated

⅛ to ¼ cup honey

pinch of cayenne

1 cup couscous, cooked according to
   package directions

nasturtium flowers

- Heat oil in pan to medium heat and sauté ginger and raisins. When raisins swell, add carrots to pan, stirring to coat carrots. Add honey and cayenne. Continue cooking, about 5 minutes more, until carrots are done.
- Remove from pan and toss with cooked couscous.
- Garnishing with nasturtium flowers on top makes a pretty dish.

Yield: 4 servings

Matzoh Charlotte   Evelyn Cutler * Elkins Park, Pennsylvania

4 matzohs

boiling water

6 egg yolks, well beaten

2 apples, cored, peeled, and cut into
  small pieces

½ cup sugar

½ cup white raisins

1 teaspoon salt

1 teaspoon vanilla

6 egg whites, beaten stiff

Wine Sauce (recipe follows)

- Preheat oven to 350°F. Grease a glass baking dish.
- Place matzohs in a colander and pour enough boiling water over the matzohs until they become mushy.
- Put matzohs in a bowl and mix in egg yolks, apples, sugar, raisins, salt, and vanilla. Fold in egg whites.
- Put mixture in baking dish.
- Bake for 30 to 45 minutes, until golden brown.
- Serve with wine sauce.

Yield: 4 to 6 servings

Wine Sauce

1 heaping teaspoon flour
1 cup sugar
4 tablespoons butter, crumbled
1 egg yolk, beaten

¾ cup wine
1 cup boiling water
1 egg white, beaten stiff

- Mix together flour, sugar, and butter. Mix in egg yolk and then slowly add wine and water. Mix together well.
- Simmer over low heat for 10 minutes.
- Remove from heat and add egg white.
- Let cool at room temperature.

In recognition of how important Jewish food is among culinary experts in this country, in 1997 the prestigious James Beard Foundation gave its top prize to *The Book of Jewish Food: An Odyssey from Samarkand to New York* written by Claudia Roden.

Ms. Roden's book is far more than a collection of recipes. It is a comprehensive journey telling just about everything there is to know about what Jews have been cooking and eating for hundreds of years in just about every part of the world.

She spent fifteen years traveling around the world eating all the foods and talking to all the people who made and ate them. Her book is almost as much a history of Jewish people throughout the world as it is a Jewish cookbook.

Liverless Chopped Liver
Debbie Besnoff * Lancaster, Pennsylvania

1 medium onion, sliced

3 tablespoons butter or margarine

3 hard-boiled eggs

½ cup walnuts

½ teaspoon salt

dash of pepper

2 tablespoons mayonnaise

crackers

- Sauté onion in butter until slightly browned. Remove from heat.
- Place onions, eggs, walnuts, salt, and pepper in a bowl and chop fine or use a food processor to grind.
- Mix in mayonnaise just before serving.
- Spread on crackers.

Yield: 4 to 6 servings

Until the late 1700s, nearly all Jews observed kosher laws. As Jews were able to leave the ghettos and move into the larger cities of Europe, there was less observance of the dietary laws.

The Reform Judaism movement that started in Germany and came to the United States in the 1800s declared that you could still be a real Jew even if you did not keep kosher.

Sweet and Sour Meatballs Gil Marshall ✳ Highland Park, New Jersey

Meatballs

3 pounds ground beef, leanest available

4 large onions, peeled and chopped

2 garlic cloves, finely sliced

4 eggs or the equivalent of Egg Beaters

pinch of salt

Sweet and Sour Sauce

2 26-ounce jars Newman's Own Venetian
Pasta Sauce

2 large onions, sliced

4 to 5 garlic cloves, thinly sliced

1 tablespoon ginger

1 cup red wine vinegar

juice and pulp of 2 lemons

¾ cup pure maple syrup

- Mix together ground beef, onions, garlic, eggs, and salt. Knead for 2 to 3 minutes, until soft and pliant.
- Wet hands with warm water and form mixture into 2- to 2½-inch balls.
- For the sauce, in a large pot thoroughly mix together pasta sauce, onions, garlic, ginger, vinegar, lemon juice and pulp, and maple syrup.
- Heat sauce to a slow boil.
- Very gradually, one by one so they do not stick together, place meatballs into sauce.
- Cover and simmer for 3 to 5 hours, stirring occasionally.
- Serve meatballs and sauce with spaghetti, wide egg noodles, or egg-free noodle dumplings.
- (This recipe is better if made a day ahead, kept in the refrigerator overnight, and then reheated and served.)

Yield: 8 to 10 servings

Jersey Brisket Helene Katzen * West Patterson, New Jersey

1 3- to 4-pound brisket

½ cup ketchup

½ cup brown sugar

1 1.2-ounce package dry onion soup mix

¾ cup water

¾ cup kosher blackberry wine

- Preheat oven to 325°F.
- Place brisket in a roasting pan.
- Combine ketchup, brown sugar, onion soup mix, water, and blackberry wine, mixing together well. Spoon over brisket in pan.
- Cover and bake for approximately 1 hour for each pound of meat. After baking for 2 hours, remove from oven and slice the brisket.
- Return sliced meat to oven and bake until done.

Yield: 8 to 10 servings

The first Dunkin' Donuts shop in Israel, located in Tel Aviv, broke the chain's world sales record selling more than three million doughnuts in less than the first twelve months it was open.

According to Asa Reshef, the Dunkin' Donuts manager of operations in Tel Aviv, "Israelis do not stop eating donuts. They buy such quantities, quantities we would have never believed they would buy. They buy boxes of twelve, eat them here, and then buy more boxes to take home."

Gary's Gravlox Gary Arenson * Davie, Florida

*rib section of a whole salmon with skin
on*
⅓ cup kosher or sea salt
½ cup sugar

3 tablespoons fresh cracked pepper
3 tablespoons chopped fresh dill
2 tablespoons liquid smoke

- Scale and fillet salmon. Cut in half lengthwise. Set aside.
- Mix together salt, sugar, pepper, dill, and liquid smoke.
- Lay one salmon fillet (skin side down) in a glass dish. Spread seasonings over fillet. Place the second fillet (skin side up) over the other fillet so it now looks like a salmon sandwich with the mixture in the middle.
- Tightly cover the dish with plastic wrap and then place a 5-pound bag of flour on top as a weight.
- Place in refrigerator and let salmon marinate for 4 days. Each day turn the fillets over and drain off any liquid that accumulates.
- After the 4 days, remove from refrigerator, rinse off the seasoning mixture, and pat dry with paper towels.
- Place the salmon skin side down on a cutting board. Slice the salmon at an angle, leaving the skin.

Yield: 4 to 6 servings

The Best Chicken Matzoh Ball Soup   Marge Rosen ✳ East Windsor, New Jersey

3 quarts water

2 teaspoons salt

½ teaspoon pepper

2 large kosher chicken breasts

6 to 8 carrots, cleaned and cut into ½-inch-thick pieces

4 to 6 stalks of celery with some of the leaves still on, broken in half

6 to 8 dill sprigs

6 to 8 parsley sprigs

1 large onion, peeled and cut in several places but not through

1 turnip, ends cut off, scraped, and cut in half

1 parsnip

1 package matzoh ball mix

1 package prepared soup noodles

- Pour water into a large pot and bring to a boil. Add salt, pepper, chicken breasts, carrots, celery, dill, parsley, onion, turnip, and parsnip.
- Cover and simmer over low heat for about 1 hour, until chicken is tender and vegetables are soft.
- Taste soup and add additional salt or pepper, if desired.
- Cook soup for an additional 15 minutes.
- Remove chicken and remove the skin and bones. Cut up chicken into small pieces.
- Remove parsnip and turnip from pot and coarsely mash them. Remove and discard onion, dill, parsley, and celery.
- Return chicken pieces and mashed parsnip and turnip to pot.
- Prepare matzoh balls according to package directions with one exception. Cook matzoh balls in salted boiling water for 10 minutes less than directions indicate.

- Transfer matzoh balls from their pot of boiling water to the soup for the last 15 minutes that the soup is cooking. Matzoh balls will absorb the juices of the soup.
- Prepare soup noodles according to package directions and add to individual bowls of soup just before serving.

Yield: 12 servings

As quintessentially Jewish as matzoh balls are, their name is relatively new.

Those dumplings made from soaked or ground up matzoh, onions, eggs, chicken fat, and spices were, up to the 1930s, usually called "klose" or "knaidlach."

In 1930, the B. Manischewitz Company published a kosher cookbook and called them "Feather Balls, Alsatian Style."

They later because popularly known as "matzoh balls" and the name has stuck.

Tzimmes
Helene Tull * Cinnaminson, New Jersey

1 12-ounce package dried pitted prunes

1 11-ounce package dried apricots

1 11-ounce package dried mixed fruit

1 12-ounce package dried figs

1 6-ounce package dried apples

1 7-ounce package dried pears

3 to 4 cinnamon sticks

1 to 2 lemons, cut into wedges

water

- Place prunes, apricots, mixed fruit, figs, apples, pears, cinnamon, and lemons in a medium-size pot. Add enough water to cover a quarter of the fruit in the pot.
- Cook over medium heat until fruit is tender and most of the water has boiled away.
- Remove from heat and chill in refrigerator.
- Serve at room temperature or reheated.

Yield: 8 to 10 servings

The first Jewish cookbook published in English was *The Jewish Manual*. It was edited by "A Lady" and made its appearance in 1846. Most of the recipes were Spanish and Portuguese along with a few German and Eastern European selections. Several recipes from England and France were also included.

Jewish Apple Cake   Barbara Freundlich * Closter, New Jersey

3 cups flour

3 teaspoons baking powder

2 cups sugar

½ pound butter, melted and cooled

4 eggs

¼ cup orange juice

2½ teaspoons vanilla

4 apples, cored, peeled, cut into wedges,
    and placed in a bowl of water to pre-
    vent browning

cinnamon sugar

- Preheat oven to 350°F. Grease and flour a 10-inch tube pan.
- Sift together flour and baking powder. Add sugar, butter, eggs, orange juice, and vanilla, beating until batter is smooth.
- Pour a third of the batter into the tube pan. Arrange a third of the apple wedges on top of the batter in the pan. Sprinkle liberally with cinnamon sugar. Pour another third of the batter on top and arrange another third of the apples wedges on top of the batter. Sprinkle again with cinnamon sugar. Repeat with the remaining batter and apple wedges. Sprinkle cinnamon sugar again.
- Bake for 1 to 1½ hours. Test after 1 hour with a fork. Cake is done when fork comes out clean.
- Remove cake from oven, set on wire rack, and let cool for 20 to 30 minutes. Place another wire rack over top of cooled cake and turn cake out. Flip cake over onto other wire rack so cake is sitting right side up.
- Let cake cool for 30 to 60 minutes more and then cover until ready to serve.
- Cake is best if made a day in advance of serving.

Yield: 6 to 8 servings

Index